Wedding Cakes

Wedding Cakes

Exciting designs with full
step-by-step instructions

Sylvia Coward

NEW
HOLLAND

First published in 1994 by
New Holland (Publishers) Ltd
London • Cape Town • Sydney • Singapore

24 Nutford Place
London W1H 6DQ
United Kingdom

80 McKenzie Street
Cape Town 8001
South Africa

3/2 Aquatic Drive
Frenchs Forest
NSW 2086
Australia

10 9 8 7 6 5 4

ISBN 1 85368 331 0 (hb)
ISBN 1 85368 293 4 (pb)

Editor: Alison Leach
Designer: Carole Perks
Photographers: Tim Frowd and Hilda Kwan
Illustrations: Gina Daniel and Stuart Perry

Typeset by Ace Filmsetting Ltd, Frome, SOmerset
Printed and bound in Malayasia
Reproduction by Hirt & Carter (Pty) Ltd
Printed and bound in Malaysia by Times Offset (M) Sdn Bhd

Contents

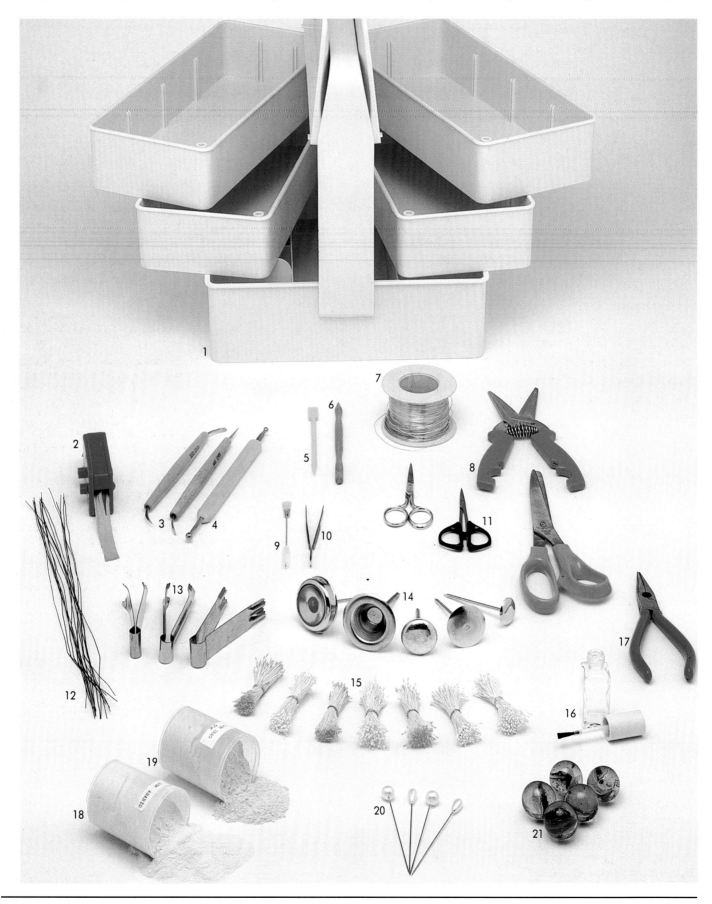

Tools and Equipment

There are certain basic tools, equipment and special ingredients which are essential for doing the various cake decorating techniques but numerous items can be added for the creation of different effects. The equipment shown in the photographs is by no means all that is available but generally covers items used for the cakes and designs featured in this book.

Although it is an advantage to have all the right tools and equipment available, you may not always have access to them. You may, therefore, find items around the house which can be used most successfully.

Auger tool: This is a most useful tool which has many uses including hollowing small flowers.

Ball tools: Various sizes of ball tools are used for modelling and moulding flowers and figures.

Brushes: A selection of good quality paintbrushes in various sizes is essential for creating special effects.

Container for egg white: A new and unused nail polish bottle and brush is most suitable for storing and applying egg white.

Crimpers: Available in a wide variety of shapes, these are used to create patterns on cakes by pinching the sugarpaste together (see page 31).

Florist or tinned copper fuse wire: This is inserted into moulded flowers to facilitate the making up of sprays. The sprays are then attached to the cake with royal icing. The wire stems should never be inserted directly into the cake.

Florist tape: This is usually available in white, brown, light and dark green and is used for taping the wires for moulded flowers.

Flower cutters: Numerous metal and plastic cutters are available for making the different flowers.

Flower formers: These are the various plastic and wooden shapes used in the making of different moulded flowers.

Flower nails: A variety of flower nails is available; the one most commonly used

consists of a flat metal or plastic disc on a spike and is used for piped royal icing flowers.

Flower stand/holder: I developed this wooden flower stand to facilitate the drying and storing of small moulded flowers.

Flower or leaf veiners: Rubber or plastic shapes that are pressed on to modelling paste to create veining on flowers and leaves.

Frill rulers: Scalloped cutters of different lengths, these are used for cutting modelling paste or pastillage to create a frilled or scalloped edge.

Gum Arabic: This can be used to glaze flowers to create a porcelain effect as well as to make edible glitter (see page 13).

Gum tragacanth: Available from specialist cake decorating shops and pharmacies, this powder is added to create the modelling paste used for making moulded flowers. It gives elasticity and is a drying agent.

Hobby or icing knife: A small knife is needed for certain types of work to cut modelling paste or pastillage.

Icing bags: For those who prefer not to use paper cones for piping, a nylon icing bag is preferable to the rigid syringe type.

Lifters: These are made from two pieces of thin board and are used for lifting the marzipan and plastic icing on to the cake.

Manicure tool: Usually found in a manicure set, this tool is used to create some animal features.

1. Workbox 2. Tape cutter 3. Modelling tools 4. Ball tool 5. Ribbon inserter 6. Auger tool 7. Fuse wire 8. Tullen scissors 9. Tube cleaning brush 10. Tweezers 11. Scissors 12. Florist wire 13. Crimpers 14. Flower nails 15. Stamens 16. Egg white container 17. Wire cutters 18. Gum Arabic 19. Gum tragacanth 20. Hatpins 21. Marbles

Moulds: Of plastic or plaster, these moulds can be filled with sugar, chocolate or modelling paste. Certain moulds are available for creating figures.

Nozzles: See Tubes.

Painting knife: This is available from art shops and is used for lifting petals, leaves, and so on.

Palette: A small plastic artist's palette with little hollows is useful for mixing colours with water or cornflour and for mixing cocoa powder with cocoa butter.

Paper cones: These are made from greaseproof paper and are generally favoured among cake decorators for use with icing tubes.

Piping jelly: Available from specialist cake decorating shops, piping jelly is a fun technique that can be used successfully on most types of icing. It holds its shape but does not set hard. It is piped around the edges of a design and then brushed towards the centre with a small, flat brush.

Ribbon inserter: This is a most useful tool with a flat shape about 10 mm (½ inch) wide on one end which is used to make slits in the icing to allow for the insertion of ribbon. The other end of the tool often has a point for creating a broderie anglaise effect, or a ridged cone for moulding flowers.

Roller: A small chrome or plastic roller is necessary for rolling out modelling paste for moulded flowers.

Rolling board: A wooden board with a melamine or other smooth covering is essential for rolling out modelling paste and pastillage.

Rolling pin: A good quality rolling pin is necessary for rolling out marzipan and sugarpaste. Personal preference is the deciding factor. A ribbed roller is very useful for creating various effects on clothes, plaques and so on.

Scissors: A good pair of small, sharp embroidery scissors is necessary for fine work.

Shears or wire cutters: These are used for cutting wire stems.

Smoothers: Two plastic rectangles used for smoothing the sides and top edges of the marzipan and sugarpaste on a cake.

Stamens: The centres of flowers require various stamens, some of which are shown in the relevant photograph.

Straight-edge cutter: Made from extruded acrylic with a sharp cutting edge, this was developed by my daughter to facilitate cutting ribbons or strips of pastillage or modelling paste.

Tape cutter: Used for cutting florist tape into four, making it possible to tape very fine wires smoothly and evenly.

Tube cleaning brush: This looks like a miniature bottle brush and is essential for easy cleaning of tubes after use.

Tubes: Sometimes also referred to as nozzles, icing tubes are available under various brand names. There is no international uniformity in the way in which they are numbered by the various manufacturers, except possibly for certain of the writing tubes. It is a good idea to select the best of each brand according to your purpose. Store the tubes carefully, standing upright, to avoid damage. The most popular tubes and tubes used on the cakes in this book are illustrated on pages 16–18.

Veining and fluting tools: These tools have curved ends and are ideal for figure and flower moulding.

Workbox: Tools and equipment need to be stored neatly and safely and the box shown here is ideal.

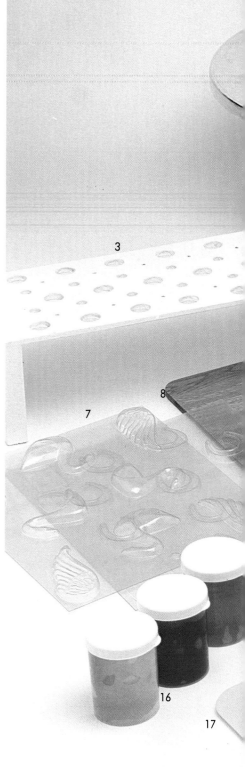

1. *Turntable* 2. *Cake board* 3. *Flower stand* 4. *Plastic rollers* 5. *Ribbed roller* 6. *Rolling pins* 7. *Plastic moulds* 8. *Pastry board* 9. *Hobby knife* 10. *Table knives* 11. *Painting knife* 12. *Craft knife* 13. *Straight-edge cutters* 14. *Frill rulers* 15. *Paper cones* 16. *Piping jelly* 17. *Smoothers* 18. *Leaf veiners* 19. *Tubes* 20. *Orchid former*

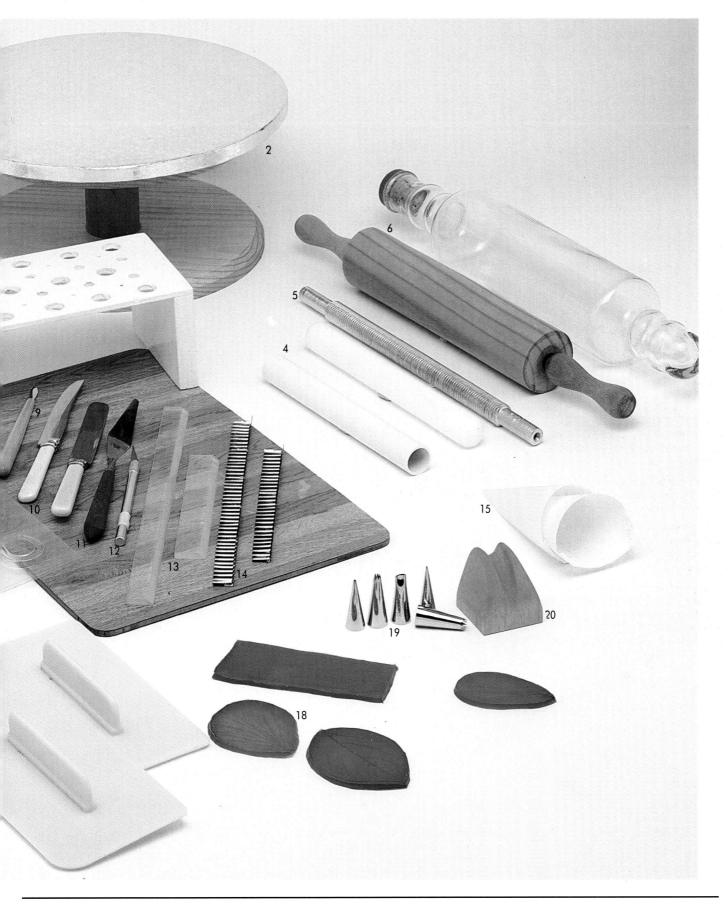

Cake Recipes

Over the years, I have received numerous requests for recipes which I have personally found successful. I have, therefore, included some of my favourites, together with a table of baking times and quantities for different shapes and sizes of cake tins.

Fruit Cake

750 g (1½ lb) mixed dried fruit
125 g (4 oz) pitted dates
125 g (4 oz) glacé cherries
125 g (4 oz) chopped nuts
125 ml (4 fl oz) brandy
250 g (8 oz) butter or margarine
250 g (8 oz) granulated sugar
6 eggs
5 ml (1 tsp) mixed spice
5 ml (1 tsp) cinnamon
2.5 ml (½ tsp) ground cloves
5 ml (1 tsp) ground ginger
30 ml (2 tbsp) golden syrup
375 g (12 oz) plain flour
5 ml (1 tsp) bicarbonate of soda

> NOTE:
> **1** Should you wish to omit the dates, increase the quantity of mixed dried fruit to 875 g (1¾ lb).
> **2** If desired, increase the quantity of mixed spice to 20 ml (4 tsp) and omit the cinnamon, cloves and ginger.
> **3** Baked cakes are approximately 75 mm (3 inches) high.

1 Soak the fruit and nuts overnight in brandy.

2 Preheat the oven to 150 °C (300 °F, gas 2).

3 Line a 225 mm (9 inch) square cake tin with greaseproof paper.

4 In a large bowl, cream the butter and sugar.

5 Add the eggs, one at a time, mixing well.

6 Add the spices and syrup.

7 Sift in the flour and continue mixing.

8 Add the fruit and nuts.

9 Mix the bicarbonate of soda with 15 ml (1 tbsp) water and add to the cake mixture. The mixture should be very thick.

10 Pour the mixture into the cake tin and bake for 2¼ hours.

11 When baked, cool the cake on a wire rack for about 30 minutes to an hour before turning out.

Chocolate Oil Cake

Butter icing is most suitable for decorating this cake.

45 ml (3 tbsp) cocoa
100 ml (3½ fl oz) boiling water
155 g (5 oz) plain flour
good pinch salt
10 ml (2 tsp) baking powder
4 eggs
185 g (6 oz) caster sugar
60 ml (4 tbsp) oil
5 ml (1 tsp) vanilla essence
2.5 ml (½ tsp) almond essence

1 Preheat the oven to 200 °C (400 °F, gas 6).

2 Grease and line two 175 mm (7 inch) sandwich tins.

3 Blend the cocoa and boiling water and allow to cool.

4 Sift together the flour, salt and baking powder.

5 Beat one egg and three yolks well, then gradually beat in the sugar and continue beating until the mixture is very thick and creamy.

6 Add the cocoa mixture, oil, vanilla and almond essence.

7 Add the flour mixture.

8 Beat the remaining egg whites until stiff peaks form and carefully fold into the cake mixture.

9 Pour the mixture into the prepared tins, tap tins gently to release the air bubbles, and bake for 25 minutes.

10 Turn out on to a wire rack to cool. When cold, fill and ice as desired.

> NOTE: This cake freezes perfectly whether decorated or plain.

Fruit, Nut and Chocolate Cake

This delicious cake does not need to be iced, but makes a valuable addition to your collection of cake recipes.

250 g (8 oz) butter or margarine
250 g (8 oz) granulated sugar
4 eggs
315 g (10 oz) plain flour
60 ml (4 tbsp) milk
125 g (4 oz) mixed dried fruit
125 g (4 oz) glacé cherries, chopped
125 g (4 oz) pecan nuts, chopped
125 g (4 oz) milk chocolate, chopped
2.5 ml (½ tsp) baking powder

1 Preheat the oven to 175 °C (350 °F, gas 4).

2 Grease and line a 325 × 100 mm (13 × 4 inch) loaf tin.

3 Cream the butter and sugar.

4 Add the eggs one at a time, beating well after each addition.

5 Sift the flour and add to the mixture together with the milk.

6 Add the dried fruit, cherries, nuts and chocolate and mix well.

7 Lastly add the baking powder.

8 Pour the mixture into the prepared tin and bake for 1½ hours.

9 Turn out on to a wire rack to cool.

Quick Sponge

Butter icing or sugarpaste can be used most successfully on this cake.

185 g (6 oz) plain flour
good pinch salt
10 ml (2 tsp) baking powder
185 g (6 oz) granulated sugar
125 g (4 oz) softened butter or margarine
2 eggs
125 ml (4 fl oz) milk
5 ml (1 tsp) vanilla essence

1 Preheat the oven to 175 °C (350 °F, gas 4).

2 Grease and flour a 200 mm (8 inch) round cake tin.

3 Sift the flour, salt, baking powder and sugar into a mixing bowl.

4 Add the butter, eggs, milk and vanilla and beat for 2 to 3 minutes with an electric mixer or for about 5 minutes by hand until well blended.

5 Pour the mixture into the prepared tin and bake for 45 minutes.

6 Turn out on to a wire rack to cool.

> NOTE: Bake cup cakes at 200 °C (400 °F, gas 6) for 10 minutes.

This recipe may help you use up some of the egg yolks you will have left over after mixing your royal icing.

Sandy Biscuits

250 g (8 oz) granulated sugar
2 eggs
3 egg yolks
315 g (10 oz) plain flour
5 ml (1 tsp) baking powder
rind of half a lemon or orange
raisins to decorate

1 Preheat the oven to 175 °C (350 °F, gas 4) and grease a baking tray.

2 Beat together the sugar, eggs and egg yolks until 'ribbons' form, about 3 minutes on fast speed.

3 Sift the flour and baking powder and add to the egg mixture together with lemon or orange rind, stirring gently.

4 Pipe long strips or rounds on to the baking tray.

5 Decorate with a raisin and sprinkle with granulated sugar.

6 Let the biscuits rest for at least 1 hour, then bake for 10 to 15 minutes.

Makes 56

Approximate Quantities of Fruit Cake Mixture and Baking Times

The following quantities of fruit cake mixture and the baking times are approximate for the sizes and shapes of the relevant tins. It is advisable always to test each cake with a cake tester or even a knitting needle to ensure that it is sufficiently baked.

Tin size and shape	Quantity	Baking time
150 mm (6 inch) square	½ × recipe	2 hours
175 mm (7 inch) square	½ × recipe	2 hours
200 mm (8 inch) square	¾ × recipe	2 hours
225 mm (9 inch) square	1 × recipe	2¼ hours
250 mm (10 inch) square	1½ × recipe	2¾ hours
275 mm (11 inch) square	2 × recipe	3 hours
300 mm (12 inch) square	2½ × recipe	3 hours
325 mm (13 inch) square	3 × recipe	3½ hours
350 mm (14 inch) square	3½ × recipe	3½ hours
150 mm (6 inch) round	⅜ × recipe	2 hours
175 mm (7 inch) round	½ × recipe	2 hours
200 mm (8 inch) round	¾ × recipe	2 hours
225 mm (9 inch) round	¾ × recipe	2 hours
250 mm (10 inch) round	1 × recipe	2¼ hours
275 mm (11 inch) round	1½ × recipe	2¾ hours
300 mm (12 inch) round	2 × recipe	3 hours
325 mm (13 inch) round	2¼ × recipe	3½ hours
350 mm (14 inch) round	2¾ × recipe	3½ hours
400 mm (16 inch) round	4 × recipe	4½ hours
150 mm (6 inch) hexagonal★	½ × recipe	2 hours
175 mm (7 inch) hexagonal	½ × recipe	2 hours
200 mm (8 inch) hexagonal	¾ × recipe	2 hours
250 mm (10 inch) hexagonal	1½ × recipe	2¾ hours
300 mm (12 inch) hexagonal	2¼ × recipe	3½ hours
350 mm (14 inch) hexagonal	3 × recipe	3½ hours
200 mm (8 inch) petal (scalloped)	½ × recipe	2 hours
250 mm (10 inch) petal	1 × recipe	2¼ hours
300 mm (12 inch) petal	1¾ × recipe	3 hours
350 mm (14 inch) petal	2½ × recipe	3½ hours
200 × 160 mm (8 × 6½ inch) oval	½ × recipe	2 hours
250 × 200 mm (10 × 8 inch) oval	1 × recipe	2¼ hours
300 × 250 mm (12 × 10 inch) oval	1½ × recipe	2¾ hours
250 × 200 mm (10 × 8 inch) rectangle	1¼ × recipe	2¾ hours
325 × 225 mm (13 × 9 inch) rectangle	2 × recipe	3 hours
150 × 150 mm (6 × 6 inch) heart	⅜ × recipe	2 hours
225 × 200 mm (9 × 8 inch) heart	¾ × recipe	2 hours
250 × 225 mm (10 × 8 inch) heart	1 × recipe	2¼ hours
300 × 265 mm (12 × 10½ inch) heart	1½ × recipe	2¾ hours
350 × 325 mm (14 × 13 inch) heart	2 × recipe	3 hours

★ NOTE: The measurements given for hexagonal-shaped tins are from side to side.

Icing Recipes

While commercially prepared marzipan, or almond paste, and sugarpaste are often available in large quantities from specialist suppliers, they may be difficult to find in country districts. I have, therefore, included the more commonly used recipes necessary to create the designs in this book.

Royal Icing

Makes about 200 g (6½ oz)

I egg white
200 g (6½ oz) icing sugar, sifted
3 drops acetic acid or 1.25 ml (¼ tsp) tartaric
acid or 2.5 ml (½ tsp) lemon juice

1 Place the egg white in a clean glass bowl and beat lightly with a wooden spoon to break up the egg white.

2 Add half the icing sugar, 30 ml (2 tbsp) at a time, beating thoroughly.

3 Add the acid or lemon juice.

4 Continue adding icing sugar 30 ml (2 tbsp) at a time, until the consistency is like well-beaten cream and holds small peaks.

5 Adjust the consistency for various types of work – a firmer texture is required for piping borders, and a softer consistency for line work.

6 When colouring royal icing, use only a touch of paste colour on the end of a cocktail stick.

> NOTE: Royal icing can be mixed with an electric mixer and will take about 5 minutes but about 15 minutes if mixed by hand.

Fondant Icing

This icing is suitable for coating cakes and for making sweets.

Makes about 1 kg (2 lb)

250 g (8 oz) liquid glucose
I kg (2 lb) icing sugar, sifted
10 ml (2 tsp) powdered gelatine
45 ml (3 tbsp) cold water
22 g (¾ oz) white vegetable fat

1 Stand the bottle of liquid glucose, with its lid off, in hot water to warm.

2 Set aside about 185 g (6 oz) icing sugar.

3 Soak the gelatine in 45 ml (3 tbsp) cold water in a small container. Place the container over hot water until the gelatine has completely dissolved.

4 Melt the fat.

5 Make a well in the remaining icing sugar and add the glucose, gelatine and fat.

6 Stir well to combine. Knead the icing and adjust the consistency by either adding some of the reserved icing sugar or egg white until a smooth pliable paste is formed.

7 Store in a plastic bag in an airtight container. Do not place in the refrigerator.

Glacé Icing

This icing sets very quickly and must be used while still warm.

Makes about 155 g (5 oz)

15 ml (I tbsp) hot water (approx)
flavouring and colouring as required
155 g (5 oz) icing sugar

1 Add the water, flavouring and colouring to the icing sugar and stir until a smooth running consistency is obtained.

2 Pour over biscuits, pastry or cakes and allow to set.

> NOTE: This quantity will cover a 175 mm (7 inch) cake or 18 cup cakes.

Butter Icing

Makes about 625 g (1¼ lb)

125 g (4 oz) butter or margarine
500 g (I lb) icing sugar
5 ml (I tsp) flavouring
small quantity of milk, water or fruit juice

1 Cream the butter thoroughly.

2 Add the icing sugar gradually.

3 Add the flavouring and beat well.

4 Add a little milk, water or fruit juice until a smooth spreading consistency is formed.

Sugarpaste

Makes about 1.5 kg (3 lb)

220 g (7 oz) granulated sugar
250 g (8 oz) liquid glucose
125 ml (4 fl oz) water
10 ml (2 tsp) powdered gelatine
flavouring and colouring (optional)
I kg (2 lb) icing sugar, sifted
22 g (¾ oz) white vegetable fat

1 Place the sugar, glucose and water in a pan and heat gently to dissolve the sugar.

2 Periodically wash down the sides of the saucepan with a wet pastry brush.

3 Bring to the boil and place the lid on for a minute or two so that the steam can wash down the sides of the saucepan.

4 Boil to 105 °C (220 °F) without stirring.

5 Soak the gelatine in 15 ml (1 tbsp) cold water.

6 Remove from the stove; when the bubbles subside add the gelatine.

7 Add the flavouring and colouring and half the icing sugar.

8 Sift the remaining icing sugar on to a large wooden or other smooth surface. Make a well in the centre and pour the mixture into it. Add the vegetable fat and

mix and knead until a smooth pliable consistency is obtained.

9 Roll out and coat the cake while the icing is still warm.

10 Store in a plastic bag in an airtight container. Do not place in the refrigerator.

> NOTE: *This icing can be reheated in a casserole in a cool oven.*

Modelling Paste 1

This paste improves with age and should be stored in an airtight container.

Makes about 500 g (1 lb)

500 g (1 lb) sugarpaste
15 ml (1 tbsp) gum tragacanth

1 Mix the sugarpaste and gum tragacanth together and knead thoroughly.

2 Store in a plastic bag in an airtight container. Do not store in the refrigerator.

3 Break off a piece of paste, dip it into egg white and knead it thoroughly before using.

Modelling Paste 2

Makes about 500 g (1 lb)

white margarine or vegetable fat
375 g (12 oz) icing sugar, sifted
25 ml (5 tsp) gum tragacanth (purest)
15 ml (1 tbsp) powdered gelatine
15 ml (1 tbsp) cold water
15 ml (1 tbsp) boiling water
1 large egg white
plastic bag

1 Grease a glass mixing bowl with white margarine or vegetable fat, add the icing sugar and place the bowl over hot water.

2 Heat the icing sugar in the bowl.

3 Add the gum tragacanth and stir with a wooden spoon to heat evenly. Do not let the sugar become moist. Heat to just warmer than blood temperature, then remove the bowl from the water.

4 Prepare the gelatine by sprinkling it on to cold water. Add the boiling water and stand the gelatine in a bowl of hot water to dissolve. Do not place it on the stove as gelatine must never get too hot.

5 Beat the egg white lightly with a fork to break it up.

6 Remove 185 g (6 oz) warm icing sugar and keep it on one side. Add the gelatine and most of the egg white to the icing sugar

in the bowl. Stir, mixing quickly and well. Add the remaining icing sugar and beat well.

7 Transfer to a clean, greased bowl and, with clean hands greased with white margarine or vegetable fat, work the paste for 10 to 15 minutes. Add the remaining egg white if the paste seems a little dry or stiff.

8 Shape the paste into a ball, grease the outside with white margarine or vegetable fat and store it in a plastic bag in a sealed container in the refrigerator.

9 Once or twice a week, take out the paste and work it for about 5 minutes.

Special Moulding Paste for Figures

Makes about 500 g (1 lb)

500 g (1 lb) sugarpaste
10 ml (2 tsp) gum tragacanth

1 Mix the gum tragacanth into the sugarpaste.

2 Allow to mature for at least a week before using. Store this modelling paste in a plastic bag in an airtight container. Do not store it in the refrigerator.

Marzipan 1

Makes about 1 kg (2 lb)

500 g (1 lb) ground almonds
250 g (8 oz) icing sugar
250 g (8 oz) caster sugar
10 ml (2 tsp) brandy
8 egg yolks

1 Mix all the dry ingredients together.

2 Add the brandy and sufficient egg yolk to make a paste. Do not knead too much as the marzipan will become oily.

3 Use immediately.

Marzipan 2

Makes about 750 g (1½ lb)

500 g (1 lb) caster sugar
250 ml (8 fl oz) water
good pinch cream of tartar
125 g (4 oz) ground almonds
1 egg, beaten
5 ml (1 tsp) ratafia or almond essence

1 Dissolve the sugar in the water over low heat.

2 Do not allow it to boil until the sugar has completely dissolved. Wash down the sides of the saucepan with a wet pastry brush.

3 Allow the mixture to boil to 120 °C (250 °F) without stirring. Remove from the heat and leave to cool for exactly 20 minutes.

4 Add the cream of tartar, almonds, egg and essence and beat with a wooden spoon until thick and creamy. Leave to cool.

5 Place the marzipan on a board and knead until smooth. Use immediately.

Pastillage

Makes about 250 g (8 oz)

250 g (8 oz) royal icing
5 ml (1 tsp) gum tragacanth
dry, sifted icing sugar

1 Mix together the royal icing and gum tragacanth. Add enough icing sugar to make a pliable dough that is no longer sticky.

2 Roll out on a board lightly dusted with cornflour and cut out the desired shapes.

3 Keep turning the shapes every few hours until evenly and thoroughly dry.

> NOTE: *Pastillage is better used at once, but can be stored in a plastic bag in an airtight container for a few hours.*

Gum Arabic Glaze
Hot water
Gum Arabic

Mix together thoroughly sufficient quantities of both to form a painting consistency. Paint on to completed moulded flowers and leaves to create a porcelain effect.

Edible Glitter
45 ml (3 tbsp) hot water
22 g (1 oz) gum Arabic

1 Pour water into a bowl and sprinkle gum Arabic over. Stand the bowl in hot water, stirring gently to dissolve. Strain mixture through a piece of nylon.

2 Brush mixture on to a clean baking tray or glass surface and place in a warm oven, 140 °C (275 °F, gas 1), until dry.

3 Brush or scrape the dry glitter off the tray and crush it into fine flakes. Store the glitter in an airtight jar.

4 Glitter may be coloured by adding colouring to the water when mixing.

Covering a Cake

The preparation of a cake prior to icing is an essential part of cake decorating. The marzipan seals the fruit cake and prevents it from staining the icing, and together the marzipan and icing form the smooth medium on to which you will pipe or mould your designs. A good base covering will make the final product look so much more professional.

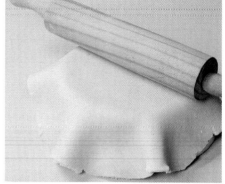

3 Bring some sieved apricot jam to a full boil. Spread the hot jam very thinly over the top and sides of the cake.

4 Sprinkle dry icing sugar on to a table top or pastry board. Roll out the marzipan until it is about 5 mm (¼ inch) thick. Use the string to check that the marzipan is large enough to cover the cake comfortably. Cut off any excess.

1 Place the fruit cake upside down on the cake board. (If the cake has risen to a hump or if it is uneven, trim it until it is level.) Knead the marzipan (page 13) until it is soft and pliable and place it in a plastic bag to prevent it drying out. Roll a thin 'sausage' of marzipan and fill any gaps between the cake and the board and any holes in the cake itself. Smooth over these and around the base of the cake with a knife until the whole surface is even.

2 Measure the distance over the cake with a length of string, starting at the base, then up one side of the cake, across the top and down to the board on the other side. Knot the string to mark the correct length.

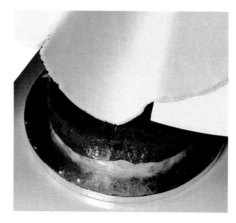

5 Slip the lifters underneath the marzipan, lift it gently and drape it over the cake. Slide out the lifters so that the marzipan falls over the cake.

6 Using a rolling pin, gently roll over the marzipan on the top of the cake and then press the marzipan against the sides of the cake with your hands.

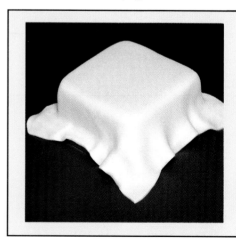

7 Trim away the excess around the base with a knife, leaving about 2.5 mm (⅛ inch) around the cake. Still using your knife, press the edges of the marzipan against the base of the cake. Rub the marzipan with both hands to smooth it, taking care not to press too hard as this will leave fingermarks. Hold a set of smoothers firmly against the sides of the cake and rub gently to smooth the marzipan further. Set the cake aside for 3 or 4 days so that the marzipan can dry out.

8 Knead and work the sugarpaste (page 12) on a pastry board, or a clean, smooth surface in the kitchen, until it is pliable. You may, if you wish, add 25 ml (5 tsp) liquid glucose to each 1 kg (2 lb) of sugarpaste to keep it soft for longer. Place the sugarpaste in a plastic bag so that it does not dry out.

9 Measure the cake with a length of string, as you did for the marzipan, and tie a knot to mark the correct measurement.

10 Place the cake in a comfortable position and dampen the marzipan (either by wetting your hands and rubbing them over the marzipan, or by using a pastry-brush dipped in water), until it is evenly covered and slightly sticky – but not wet and syrupy. Wipe off any water on the board.

11 Sprinkle the working surface with dry icing sugar. Place the sugarpaste on the icing sugar and roll it out, lifting it occasionally and keeping it to the shape of the cake. Do not turn the icing over. When the icing is of an even thickness, use the string to check that you have the correct size and cut away any excess. Give the icing a good 'polish' with your hands and prick any air bubbles that have emerged.

To cover a square cake
1 Lay the sugarpaste over the cake, making sure it will cover the entire cake comfortably.

2 Once the top is flat, smooth and fit the corners by cupping your hand around each corner before doing the sides.

To cover a plain cake
To cover a plain cake with sugarpaste, spread the cake with smooth apricot jam but omit the marzipan.

Assembling tiers using plastic pillars

1 Once the cake has been covered with sugarpaste, work out the position of the pillars. Make a template from paper or thin card by drawing around the cake tin. Fold the template into quarters to find the centre.

2 Mark the position of the pillars on the template by measuring the distance diagonally from the centre. Place the template on the cake and mark the positions with a pin. Remove the template.

Size of cake	Distance of pillar from centre
200 mm (8 inch)	65mm (2½ inches)
250 mm (10 inch)	75 mm (3 inches)
300 mm (12 inch)	90 mm (3½ inches)

3 Carefully push a skewer into the cake until the point reaches the cake board. Place the pillar next to the skewer and mark the skewer level with the top of the pillar. Carefully remove the skewer and use this as a measure to cut the remaining skewers to the same length. Insert cut skewers, blunt-end first, into the cake. Place the pillars over the skewers.

Assembling tiers using extruded acrylic stands

1 Place a square or circle of paper over the stand and mark the centre of the pillars on the paper.

2 Place the paper in the centre of the covered cake and mark the positions of the pillars on the cake with a pin. Remove the paper.

3 Insert the pointed end of a skewer into the cake at each of the marked spots until the skewer touches the cake board. Remove the skewer, then re-insert it, blunt-end first, into one of the holes. With a pencil, mark the skewer level with the top of the cake, then remove the skewer and cut it at the marked spot. Cut more skewers to the same length.

4 Place a cut skewer into each of the holes in the cake. The skewers should be about 1 mm (¹⁄₁₆ inch) below the surface of the cake. Conceal the ends of the skewers with a little royal icing or sugarpaste. Place the extruded acrylic stand on the cake so that the pillars are positioned above each skewer.

12 Slide your hands or the lifters under the sugarpaste and lift it on to the cake, checking to see that the icing covers the entire surface of the cake.

13 Now, using your hands, gently ease the sugarpaste around the cake (if it is a square cake, start with the corners first) without making folds in the icing or tearing it. While you are working, gently rub your hands all over the cake to give a smooth, satiny finish. Trim away any excess icing at the base of the cake.

14 Use a smooth knife and firmly press the icing against the base to give a smooth, even finish.

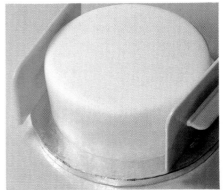

15 Check all around the cake and smooth over any uneven patches. Use smoothers to even the sides of the cake further.

NOTE: *Approximately 1 kg (2 lb) each of sugarpaste and marzipan is required to cover a 250 mm (10 inch) cake.*

Decorating Techniques

Tubework or piping is an essential part of cake decorating. With practice, you will soon master the fine art of decorating a cake using royal icing and a tube. The following pages will take you step by step through the various basic techniques such as lines, loops, shells, scrolls, embroidery, lace pieces, basket weave and so on. In addition, full colour, step-by-step photographs illustrate simply and clearly the techniques of piping flowers as these are an integral part of this decorative art form.

 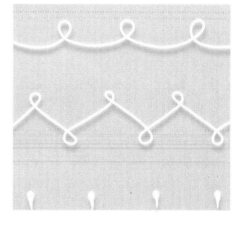

EXERCISES ON GLASS

It is very useful to practise on a sheet of glass as it is easy to keep clean and enables you to make certain of mastering a step or technique before working on an actual cake. Later on, when you begin to learn more difficult designs, a pattern can be placed under the glass which you can follow while working on top.

ICING TUBES

Writing tubes: These are used for writing messages on to cakes, making dots, lines, loops, embroidery (page 20) and also for figure piping (page 29). Generally, these tubes are the lower numbers in the range, for example 00, 0, 1, 2, and so on.

A very useful exercise for piping *lines* and *loops* is to touch the work surface with the end of the tube, press on the cone and then lift the tube about 35–40 mm (1½–1¾ inches) away from the glass or cake, pressing constantly and not stretching the icing, so that the icing falls into place on the surface.

When forming *dots* and *beads*, it is difficult to disguise the tail. For small dots, the icing should be soft. Use very little pressure on the cone, just enough to make a tiny dot. For larger dots use constant pressure and keep the point of the tube stationary in the bead or dot until it is the size required. Release pressure and move the cone gently in a circle before removing the tube. Gently press any projecting point down into the dot or bead, if necessary.

Cornelli or scribbling is done with No. 00, 0 or 1 writing tubes using a maze of Ws and Ms in a continuous line but at random. You should not be able to see where the work begins or ends.

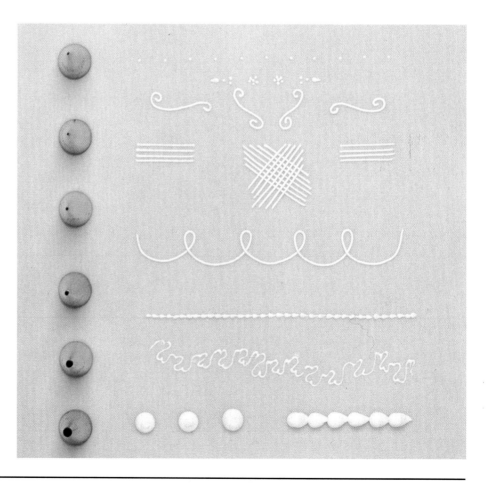

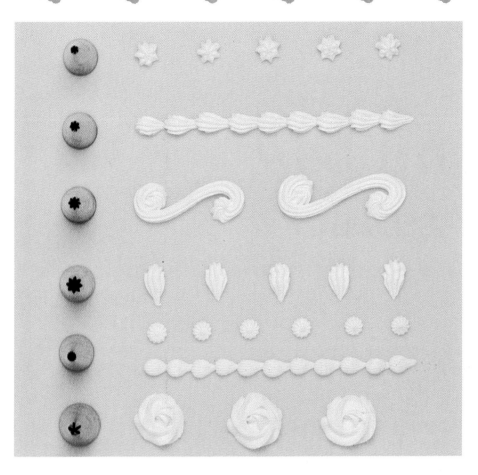

Star tubes: There is a very large range of star tubes available. These are used for making shells, stars, scrolls and so on. Make sure the icing is the correct consistency – it should form a firm peak when a knife is lifted out of the icing.

To create *stars*, hold the cone, fitted with the appropriate tube, perpendicular to the surface. Press the cone firmly to release the icing, stop pressing, then remove the cone.

To form *shells*, use any of the star tubes available and hold the icing cone at a 45 ° angle. With the tip of the tube touching the surface of the work, press very firmly. Move the tube slightly away from the surface giving the icing room to build up. Ease off pressing, then stop pressing, tapering off the icing by pulling the cone towards you. You have now formed the first shell. Now, just touching on the end of the first, start the next shell, ensuring that the untidy start of the icing does not show and again, pressing very firmly, repeat the procedure.

To create *pull-up shells* around the side of a cake, repeat the same procedure in an upwards direction.

Rosettes are piped with a deep-cut star tube, that is either a Probus No.13 or Ateco No. 33, moved in a circular motion.

Petal tubes: These can be either straight, such as Probus No. 42 or Ateco No. 101, or curved, such as the Bekenal No. 57, and are used for any royal icing flowers such as roses, daisies, and so on. An exception is the horseshoe shape, Ateco No. 81, used for chrysanthemums and lily-of-the-valley. (See pages 26–28 on how to pipe different flowers.)

Drop flower tubes, which make a whole flower with one pressing of the icing cone, are also available in many varieties, for example Probus No. 31 and Ateco No. 224. My favourite is the Bekenal No. 37 drop flower tube as it is very easy to use (see page 27 for details).

Special effect tubes: For a shell and ruffle border, the Ateco Nos. 86, 87 and 88 are very effective. The grass or hair tube, Ateco No. 233, is also very useful. Multiple hole tubes can be used most successfully in various ways, for example there is one with five holes in a row which can be used for writing music lines on a cake.

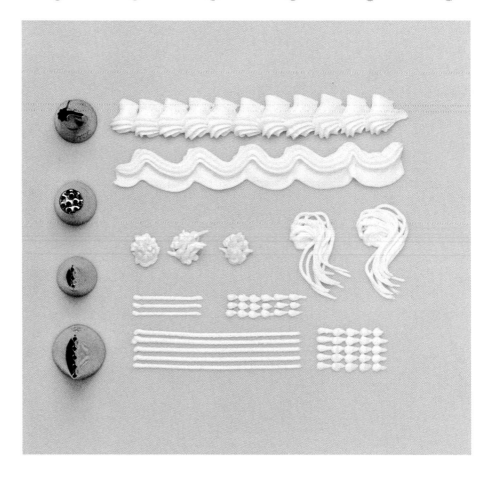

Ribbon tubes: One or both edges are serrated and these can be used for piping ribbons or bands and also for basket weave, for example Bekenal No. 22. Included here is the curved tube, Ateco No. 98 (sometimes referred to as a shell tube) which is the one I like to use for basket weave (page 24).

Leaf tubes: While one can use a paper cone to pipe leaves, there are very good leaf tubes available in three sizes, namely the Ateco Nos. 349, 350 and 352.

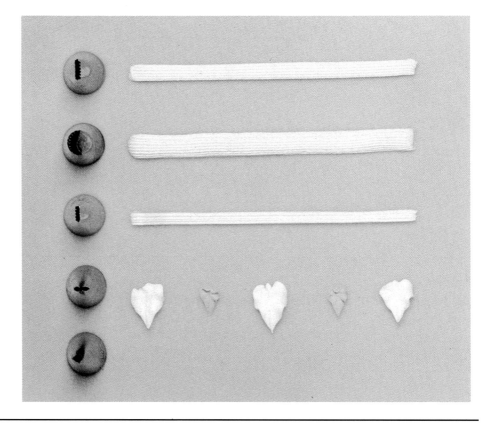

FLOODWORK

Floodwork, or run-in-work, is the art of filling in a picture with royal icing thinned to the right consistency. It is advisable to do more than one picture at a time so that, while one section is drying, you can work on a section in another picture. Floodwork items will keep very well in a strong box protected from dust and bumps.

Mix royal icing to a firm peak consistency and then thin down half of it with a few drops of water. Use an eye dropper to get the consistency exactly right. Do not beat the icing when adding the water but stir it gently. It is preferable to allow the icing to stand for 12 hours so that any bubbles can subside.

When a knife is drawn through it, the thinned icing should only come together after a slow count of ten. Icing which is too thin does not set well.

It is important to dry floodwork quickly to retain its shine. If you are working on a rainy day, use a heater or the warming drawer to dry it.

1 Place the picture to be flooded under glass and stick it in place at the corners with a little royal icing. Tape a piece of waxed (not greaseproof) paper to the glass, ensuring that there is at least a 25 mm (1 inch) margin around the edge of the picture. Do make sure that there are no wrinkles in the paper. If the design has a middle opening (like a collar, for example) you may cut a small cross in the centre of the paper to relax the natural tension of the paper. Any buckling or wrinkling of the paper may cause the design to break.

2 Outline the picture using firm peak royal icing in a small writing tube.

3 Fill a paper cone with thinned icing, but do not cut the hole in the bottom until you are ready to fill in the design otherwise the icing will flow out. It is not necessary to use a tube. Make sure the hole is not too big, or the icing may flow out too quickly, overrunning your lines. Start close to your outline, but do not touch it with the cone as it may break. Always start filling in the part of the picture that is furthest away from you. For example, of two trees one behind the other, you would do the back one first.

Keep the tip of the bag close to the surface to reduce the formation of air bubbles and let the icing flow out, moving the bag backwards and forwards across the shape.

4 When flooding a collar for a cake, flood a section and then flood alternately on either side of that section. This prevents the icing from setting and leaving a line.

5 When the area is almost filled, use a small paintbrush to push the icing to the outline to form a smooth edge. If any bubbles appear, immediately smooth them away with a paintbrush or hatpin.

6 Once the floodwork is dry, slide the piece of paper with the floodwork on to the edge of the table. Gently pull the paper downwards against the edge of the table while supporting the floodwork with your other hand. Keep turning the picture so that the paper is removed evenly all round. Do not extend the floodwork more than 50 per cent beyond the table edge.

7 To attach a collar, pipe a line of icing with a No. 2 writing tube all around the top edge of the cake and then position the collar on this line. When positioning smaller pieces on a cake, it is easier to paint the back of the floodwork piece with royal icing before attaching it.

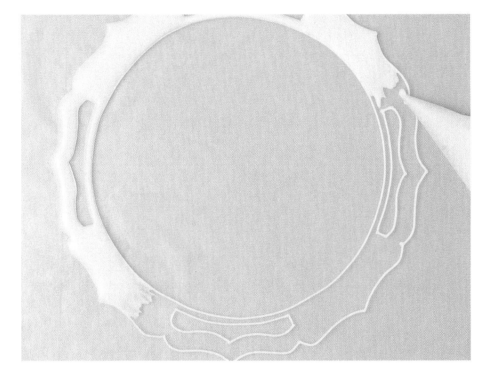

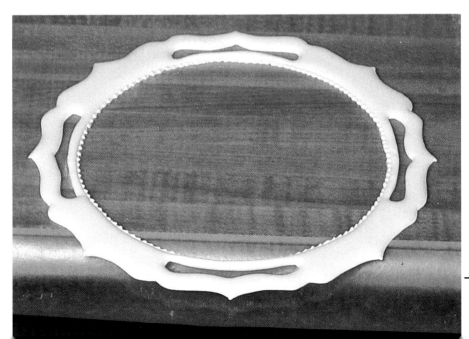

EMBROIDERY

The fine designs piped on to the side of a cake are commonly called 'embroidery'. This is best done with one of the fine writing tubes and royal icing with a 'soft peak' consistency.

The design can be done free-hand on the cake or, if you wish, pricked out using a tracing. This latter method has its disadvantages, however, as the pinpricks will show. The method I use is to prick only the centres of the little flowers and then add the stems and leaves. Another method is to use a glass stencil (page 24) to transfer the design on to fresh icing.

It is advisable to make a very simple embroidery design on the cake initially and later, when you feel more confident, to try a more complicated design. Patterns for various embroidery designs can be found on page 70.

1 Fill a small writing tube with royal icing and pipe the embroidery design by first piping the centre dot of each flower.

2 Then pipe the five dots around each centre, and lastly, the stems and leaves.

Picot Edge

1 Fill a No. 0 or 1 writing tube with royal icing and pipe a row of small dots.

2 Pipe three dots opposite the spaces next to the first four dots.

3 Pipe two dots opposite the spaces next to the three dots and then one dot between the two dots.

4 Miss one dot in the original row of dots and repeat Steps 2 and 3 to create the picot effect.

Brush Embroidery

This interesting and effective technique uses royal icing to which a little water has been added or, alternatively, 2.5 ml (½ tsp) piping jelly, liquid glucose or glycerine may be added to one mixture of royal icing.

The glass stencil method is ideal for transferring the design on to the cake but, to avoid a mirror image of your design, trace on to the back of the pattern and then follow that with royal icing in a No. 0 writing tube.

1 Fill a No. 1 or 2 writing tube with the royal icing and with extra pressure, pipe a line around a petal or leaf.

2 Hold a 2.5 mm (⅛ inch) wide flat brush at an angle of about 45 ° and brush the icing from the outer edge inwards. Follow the veins of the petals or leaves. Leave the outer edge thicker, fading away to the centre or lower point.

3 Work on a small section at a time to prevent the icing from drying before you have brushed it. Small details, such as dots for stamens, may be piped in afterwards once the brush embroidery has set.

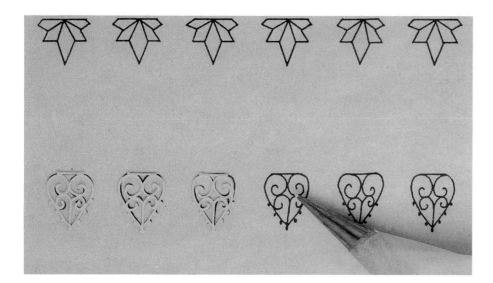

LACE PIECES

Because they are so fragile and break easily, lace pieces are usually the last decoration to be added to a cake. Patterns of various lace pieces can be found on page 71.

1 Copy the design on to a piece of tracing paper using a sharp pencil or fine felt-tip pen.

2 Tape the four corners of the tracing paper to a work surface and tape a larger piece of waxed paper over the pattern. Use only a couple of pieces of tape so that you do not disturb the lace pieces too much when you remove the tape.

3 Pipe the lace pieces on to the waxed paper using a small writing tube. Wipe the end of the tube with a damp cloth while piping each piece to ensure clean lines. Always make more pieces than are needed to allow for breakages. Allow the pieces to dry for at least 2 hours.

4 Remove the lace by placing the waxed paper over the index finger of your left hand. The lace will start to lift. Gently lift it off between the thumb and forefinger. Do not attempt to lift the lace pieces off with tweezers as the slightest pressure will break them.

5 Use a small writing tube to make a 25 mm (1 inch) row of dots on the cake. Press the straight edge of the lace piece into the centre of the dots to secure it. Continue to attach the other lace pieces in the same way, then gently push each piece so that it slopes slightly downwards.

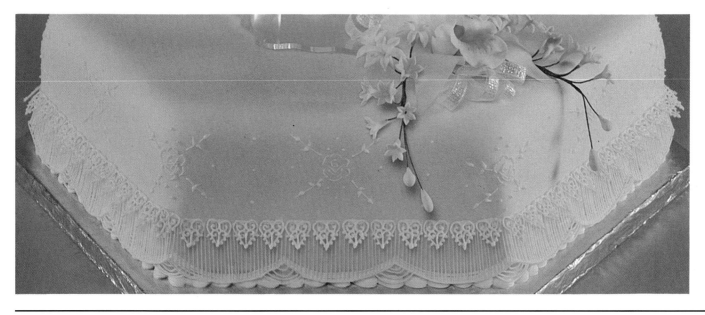

EXTENSION WORK

This is a method of bordering a cake. The depth of regular or basic extension work should be about one-third of the height of the cake or about 35 mm (1½ inches) deep. It is advisable not to make the extension work too deep to start with as the longer the lines, the more difficult they are to do.

1 Cut a strip of greaseproof paper as wide as the depth of your cake and as long as its circumference. Draw two pencil lines along the length of the paper 35 mm (1½ inches) and 10 mm (½ inch) from one edge.

2 Fold the paper in half by putting the two ends together, then fold again and continue in this way until the paper is folded into a piece about 30 mm (1¼ inches) wide. Open out the paper strip and put it around the cake with the 10 mm (½ inch) line close to the cake board and then stick the ends together with sticky tape. On a square cake, see that there is a fold of the paper on each corner. Now make a pinprick at 35 mm (1½ inches) and 10 mm (½ inch) on each fold line round the cake.

3 Remove the greaseproof paper and rule a line on the cake with a pin, joining together the upper pinpricks. At this point embroidery is done on the sides of the cake.

4 Fill a writing tube (any size from 00 to 3) with royal icing (the icing should be the same consistency used for making shells) and make a continuous row of beading around the base of the cake where it meets the board. Allow to set.

5 Fill a writing tube (any size from 00 to 3) with royal icing and pipe the first 'support row' by touching the tube to the first of the 10 mm (½ inch) pinpricks. Move to the next 10 mm (½ inch) pinprick, pressing the cone and letting the icing fall into a scallop between the marks. Taper off each scallop at the beginning and end so that the icing is not too thick. Continue in this way right around the cake.

It is absolutely essential that you do not let the icing scallops touch the board. Any movement in the board could crack the extension work and a whole section could be damaged. Allow this first row of scallops to dry partially for about 30 minutes.

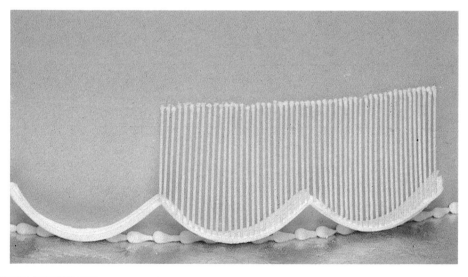

6 Do another support row of scallops by piping directly on to the first row. When you look at the scallops at eye level, they should appear as a single line.

7 When the second row of scallops is complete, allow it to firm before adding the third row of scallops. Additional rows of scallops may be added, if desired. (Adding a new row while the previous one is still wet may make the whole lot collapse.) Leave for about 24 hours to allow these support rows to dry thoroughly before continuing the extension work.

8 Using a small writing tube, pipe a line from the 35 mm (1½ inch) line to a point where two scallops meet. Then pipe a line to the deepest point of the scallop and a third line to the point where this scallop

joins the next one. Then, pressing firmly, pipe a series of lines from the 35 mm (1½ inch) line to the edge of the scallop – make sure that each line remains taut. The space between the drop lines should be the width of a line – you should not be able to fit more than one line between the drop lines. Continue in this way right around the cake.

9 With the same tube, pipe a line over the end of the drop lines on the scallop to neaten off the base of the extension work.

> *NOTE: If the icing keeps breaking, the reason may be either that you are not pressing firmly and consistently on the cone, or that the icing is too soft – it is very important to have your icing the correct consistency. Finally, the icing may be too stiff, in which case add a few drops of water or egg white or, preferably, mix a fresh batch.*

GLASS STENCILS

I have found this technique invaluable for transferring embroidery designs, lettering or pictures on to a cake.

1 Trace the design on to a piece of paper. Carefully outline the design on the back of the paper with a pencil.

2 Place the design under the glass so that the pencilled outlines are facing you. Fill a paper cone with royal icing and, using a small writing tube, pipe directly on to the glass (the lettering or design will be back-to-front). Allow the icing to dry.

3 When the icing is quite hard, press the design against fresh sugarpaste. Lift the glass away and you will have the design on your cake exactly where you want it.

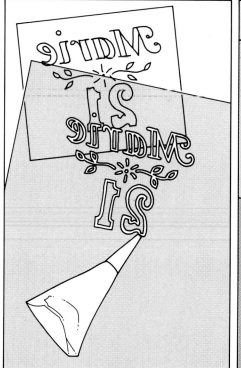

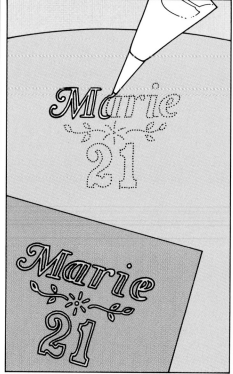

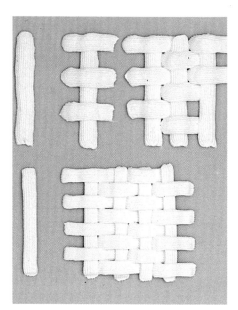

BASKET WEAVE

Weaving is achieved by using a ribbon tube (where one edge is serrated and the other straight) and royal icing.

1 Pipe a vertical line the required length on to the work surface, then do a number of short lines across the first vertical line, leaving a space the width of your tube between them.

2 Now do another vertical line, just covering the ends of the short ones.

3 Pipe short lines over this vertical line so that the start of your short line looks as though it is coming from underneath the first long vertical line. Continue in this way, filling in all the spaces along the last vertical line. Repeat this procedure until you have covered the area required.

ROPING

1 Fill a cone with royal icing and use a small or medium star tube, or a large writing tube, to create a twisted rope. Hold the cone at a 45 ° angle and pipe a 'comma' curving downwards, then to the left, flicking slightly to the right as you end off. Keep constant pressure on the cone as you work.

Right: The two shades of brown royal icing used in this basket weave pattern look most effective.

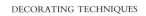

PIPED FLOWERS

Unfortunately, since the popularity of moulded flowers, piped flowers have lost much of their glamour. This is a great shame as they are fun to make, involve a certain amount of skill and, apart from that, can be attractively used in a variety of ways to decorate pastillage cards, ornaments and plaques for wedding cakes.

Apple Blossom Flower, Bud and Leaf

Equipment
medium petal tube
white, pink and green royal icing (page 12)
small writing tube or plain cone
40 mm (1¾ inch) square waxed paper
flower nail

1 Fill a medium petal tube with pink and white icing, placing the pink icing on the side of the cone to line up with the wider opening of the petal tube and then adding the white icing. Fill a small writing tube, or a plain cone cut to size, with green icing. Fix a small square of waxed paper to the top of the flower nail with a touch of icing.

Blossom
1 Hold the flower nail in your left hand (right if left-handed). In the other hand, hold the tube of pink and white icing at an angle of about 30° to the surface of the nail with the wider opening, where the pink icing is, to the centre of the nail. The narrow opening in the tube must be slightly raised from the nail.

2 Press the cone, moving the tube very slightly towards the outer edge of the nail and at the same time, turning the nail very slightly in an anti-clockwise direction (clockwise for left-handers). Now move the tube back towards the centre of the nail and stop turning and pressing. This is the first petal of the apple blossom which has five petals.

3 Repeat four more petals, starting each new petal slightly under the preceding one. Take care with the last petal and lift the cone, not the tube, slightly higher, to about a 45° angle, so as not to damage the previous petals.

4 Use the cone containing the green icing and pipe five very small dots close to each other in the centre of the complete flower.

5 Remove the waxed paper very carefully from the flower nail. Hold a corner between thumb and forefinger and then slide the middle finger underneath the paper to support the flower. Place it in a box or on a piece of glass to dry.

Bud (or slightly opened flower)
1 Pipe three petals as you did for the blossom flower.

2 Turn the flower nail so that the three petals are facing you upside down. With a small writing tube filled with green icing, pipe a teardrop starting from the base of the first petal and finishing close to the top of the petal. Repeat on the other two petals to form the calyx.

3 Turn the nail so that the petals are the right way up. Place the tube into the base of the calyx and press very firmly to form a bulb, then taper away into a stem.

NOTE: To make a smaller bud, make only two petals and do exactly the same as described above. These buds help to 'soften' the arrangement of flowers on a cake.

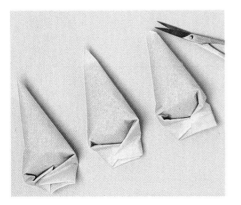

Leaf
1 Fill a plain cone with green royal icing and cut the cone to form a leaf shape. A leaf tube can also be used.

2 Press firmly and allow the icing to build up. Reduce pressure and pull the tube away, tapering the end of the leaf.

NOTE: These leaves can be made in advance and allowed to dry or they can be piped directly on to a cake and used to attach the royal icing flowers.

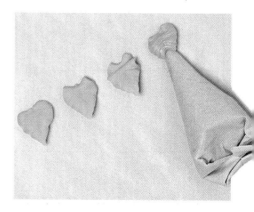

Daisy

Two types of daisy can be piped.

Equipment
white and yellow royal icing (page 12)
medium petal tube
small writing tube
40 mm (1¾ inch) square waxed paper
flower nail

1 Colour a quarter of the icing yellow. Fill a cone with a medium petal tube and white royal icing and another with a small writing tube and yellow icing. Attach a square of waxed paper to the flower nail with a dot of royal icing.

Method 1

1 With the medium petal tube and white icing, pipe a series of petals as you did for the apple blossom, but make each petal slightly longer. Do not forget that the wider opening in the tube must be facing towards the centre of the nail. The daisy can have any number of petals.

2 Make a large dot in the centre of the flower using the small writing tube and yellow icing. Remove the flower and the waxed paper square from the nail and set it aside to dry.

DROP FLOWERS

Drop flowers, most suitable for use on children's cakes, are piped in one action using a special tube. A Bekenal No. 37 tube is my favourite.

1 Hold the cone of icing, with the tube in it, at right angles close to the work surface. Press so that enough icing shows to form an attractive flower. Stop pressing before lifting the tube away from the icing.

2 Pipe centres with yellow icing in a small writing tube and pipe the leaves with a paper cone cut to shape or use a leaf tube.

> NOTE: Some drop flowers require a twist of the wrist as one is pressing the cone.

Method 2

1 Hold the tube containing white icing just above the surface of the nail and at right angles to it, with the wider opening in the tube towards the centre of the nail. Start about 10 mm (½ inch) from the centre of the nail and press firmly, moving the tube to the centre of the nail. Continue in this way, working in a circle. Any number of petals may be used for this flower, but they must be of even thickness and close together. Take care not to 'stretch' the icing as this results in thin petals which break very easily when removed from the waxed paper. Do not turn the flower nail when piping a petal of this flower.

2 When the petals are complete, pipe a yellow dot in the centre of the flower using the writing tube. Remove the flower and the waxed paper from the nail and set it aside to dry.

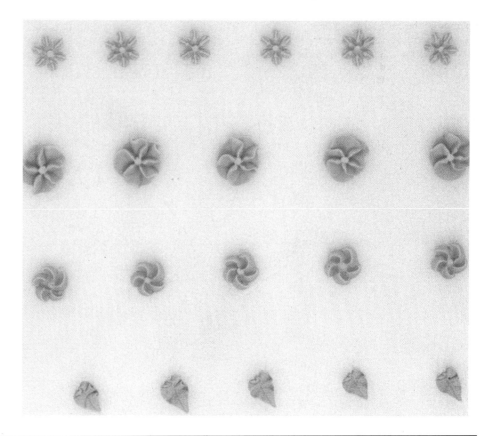

Rose Flower and Bud

Equipment
40 mm (1¾ inch) square waxed paper
flower nail
large petal tube
250 ml (8 fl oz) pale pink royal icing (page 12)

NOTE: The rose can be piped directly on to a cocktail stick instead of on to a flower nail. Touch the end of the cocktail stick in some white margarine or vegetable fat and then pipe the rose directly on to it. Remove gently when the flower has set.

1 Attach the waxed paper to the flower nail with a dot of royal icing. Fill a large petal tube and a paper cone with pale pink icing.

2 Hold the tube against the waxed paper on the flower nail and at right angles to it. With the wide end of the tube to the centre of the nail, press the cone, and when the icing comes through, pull the cone towards you as though you are pulling down a lever. When the side of the tube is touching the nail, turn the nail in your left hand (right hand if left-handed) in a clockwise direction (anti-clockwise if left-handed) allowing the icing to wrap around the icing already on the nail, thus forming a cone.

3 End off by turning the nail but holding the tube steady in the one position until you have completely circled the cone. Stop pressing and turn the nail and pull the tube away in the same direction ending low on the cone and close to the nail.

4 Continue building this cone of icing by wrapping another 'band' of icing around the icing on the nail. Hold the paper cone at a 45 ° angle with the tube close to the top of the icing on the nail and almost touching it. This cone will form the centre of the rose. Repeat this process once more so that the cone is 15 mm (¾ inch) high.

5 Touch the wide end of the tube to the flower cone about halfway up, with the narrow part of the tube towards your left and away from the icing. Press and turn your right hand from the wrist to the right in an 'up and over' movement, rather like opening a fan. Pipe two more in this way.

6 Hold the tube in the same position as for the first three petals, but start at the base of the cone, in line with the centre of the first petal, right against the nail. Move up and over, turning your hand from the wrist from left to right and finish the petal in line with the centre of the next petal of the previous row. Pipe two more petals in the same way.

7 You have now completed the rose. Carefully remove the waxed paper and rose from the nail and set it aside to dry thoroughly.

Rosebud
1 Proceed as for the rose flower, but after the first three petals shake the nail gently so that the cone falls on to its side and the 'V' formed by two of the petals is facing you.

2 Use a hatpin to cut away the excess icing on either side of the base of the bud.

FIGURE PIPING

Figure piping may be executed with any size writing tube but, of course, the size of the tube will determine the size of the figure. Use royal icing that is firm enough to hold its shape when piped into a ball but not so stiff as to form ridges. No patterns are required for these amusing motifs as figure piping is done freehand. Use constant pressure and keep the end of the tube in the icing while piping.

Tiny teddy bear: Use a No. 0 writing tube and royal icing and pipe the body, head, arms, legs and ears, in that order, on to a piece of waxed paper. When the teddy is dry, remove it and attach it to the cake with royal icing.

Bunny: Using white royal icing in a No. 2 writing tube, pipe the bunny as shown on to waxed paper and leave it to dry. Remove the bunny and attach it to the cake with royal icing.

Baby face: Pipe the face on to waxed paper with soft flesh-coloured royal icing in a No. 3 or 4 writing tube and allow it to dry

thoroughly. Paint the eyes and mouth with food colouring. With white royal icing in a No. 3 or 4 writing tube, pipe a large ball on to waxed paper to form the bonnet. Immediately attach the face by pushing it into this ball. If desired, trim the bonnet with tiny royal icing dots using a No. 0 or 1 writing tube and leave it to dry thoroughly.

RIBBON BOWS

Ribbon bows made from florist ribbon are very useful decorations for celebration cakes. They are usually made from strips of ribbon about half a metre (yard) long and of any width. Make a few bows in different sizes and colours and keep them ready for use.

1 Cut a length of ribbon 500 mm (20 inches) long and 10 mm (½ inch) wide. At one end make a loop about 30 mm (1¼ inches) long so that the end hangs below the short one.

2 Fold the long end so that the right side is uppermost, then make another loop to form the other half of the bow.

3 Fold underneath again so that the right side is uppermost and continue until no more loops can be made.

4 Cut a length of wire about 50 mm (2 inches) long and bend it over the centre of the ribbon to hold the latter firmly together, then twist the wire tightly.

5 Pull the loops so that they all point in the same direction.

6 Curl the loose end of the bow using the blade of a pair of scissors. Attach the bow to the cake with royal icing, by inserting it into a small mound of sugarpaste or by taping it to flower sprays.

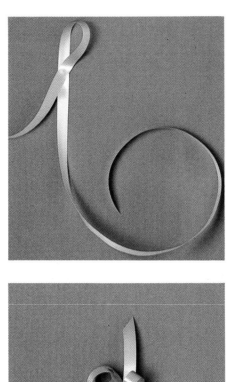

RIBBON INSERTION

Ribbon insertion is used very effectively with embroidery and as an attractive side decoration on cakes.

It is important to cut the ribbon slots while the sugarpaste is still fresh.

1 Cut a piece of greaseproof paper the same height as the cake and long enough to go right around the cake. Join the ends together with tape and slip it off the cake.

2 Flatten the paper and press in the folds so that the paper is double.

3 Fold the paper in half lengthwise, then open it up and draw a pencil line along this fold.

4 Now draw two more lines, one about 5 mm (¼ inch) above the centre line and one 5 mm (¼ inch) below.

5 Measure the length of the paper and mark even spaces with pencil dots along the centre pencil line.

6 Replace the paper around the cake and, with a pin, carefully make two pin-pricks on the top and bottom lines in line with the pencil dots.

7 Remove the paper and cut vertical slots into the sugarpaste with a ribbon inserter (or hobby knife) to join the pin-pricks.

There are several methods of inserting ribbons. Here are four examples.

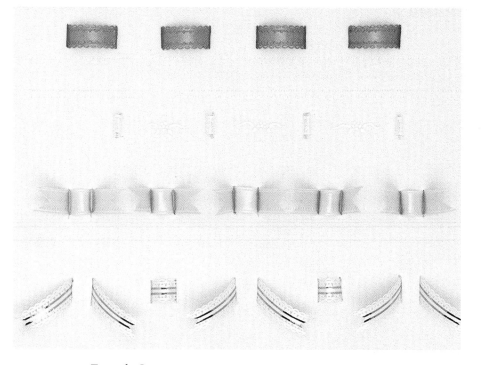

Example A

1 Use 10 mm (½ inch) wide ribbon and cut it into 25 mm (1 inch) long pieces.

2 With the ribbon inserter, cut slots into the sugarpaste at about 25 mm (1 inch) intervals.

3 Slot a piece of ribbon into every alternate space.

Example B

1 Use 10 mm (½ inch) wide very soft, satin ribbon and cut it into 20 mm (¾ inch) long pieces.

2 Cut slots at 25 mm (1 inch) intervals with a ribbon inserter. Bend the ribbon in half and insert both ends into the same slot.

Example C

1 Cut 10 mm (½ inch) wide ribbon into 50 mm (2 inch) lengths and cut a 'V' out of each end.

2 Cut pairs of slots into the icing anything from 5–10 mm (¼–½ inch) apart with a space of 25mm (1 inch) between them.

3 Insert the ribbon into the two slots, leaving approximately 20 mm (¾ inch) of the ends showing.

Example D

1 Cut 10 mm (½ inch) wide ribbon into 35 mm (1½ inch) lengths and cut a 'V' out of one end. Cut the other end at an angle. Cut 12 mm (⅝ inch) lengths of the same ribbon.

2 Cut pairs of slots into the icing 10 mm (½ inch) apart at 25 mm (1 inch) intervals. Insert the pieces of ribbon into the prepared slots.

SUGAR MOULDING

This is one of the simplest of cake decorating techniques that produces delightful results.

Ingredients
375 g (12 oz) caster sugar
20 ml (4 tsp) water

1 Mix the caster sugar and water together thoroughly with a fork to ensure that there are no lumps.

2 Spoon the mixture into the mould, press down well, then turn out. Tap gently on the top if necessary, to release it.

> NOTE: To colour the sugar, add a few drops of food colouring to the water before mixing it with the sugar.

CRIMPING

This is a method of creating patterns by pinching sugarpaste together with the use of a crimper. Crimpers come in several designs, but two of the most pleasing and easy to use are the V-shape and the single scallop.

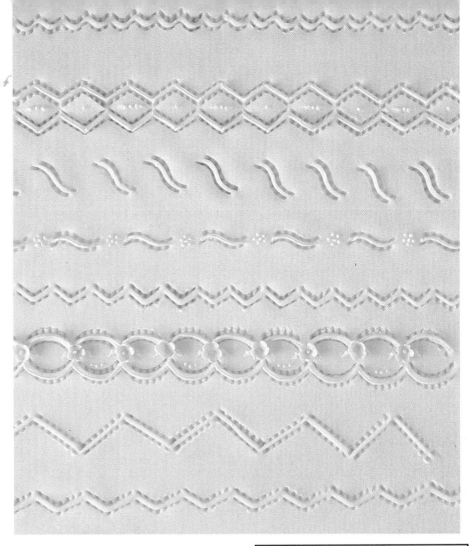

When doing crimping work, especially on a square cake, measure the edge along which you are going to crimp and divide it by the width of the crimper to check that the row will fit perfectly. Always work on freshly applied sugarpaste. The crimper ends must be held close together to avoid long 'drag' lines when you pinch the icing. Crimping should always be finished off with royal icing.

1 Dip the ends of the crimper into cornflour. Hold the crimper between thumb and forefinger, with your middle finger as a guide. The ends should be about 5 mm (¼ inch) apart.

2 Insert the crimper into the icing. Press the ends together until there is about 2.5 mm (⅛ inch) between them. Open the crimpers slightly and remove them.

3 Keep dipping the ends of the crimper in cornflour to prevent them sticking to the icing. Continue in this way along the section you wish to crimp. Decorate with royal icing.

> NOTE: If you have difficulty in holding the ends of the crimper close together, put a strong elastic band around the crimper to keep the ends about 5 mm (¼ inch) apart.

1 Fill a bell mould, or metal or plastic Christmas bell with the clapper removed, with the sugar mixture. Pack it in firmly. Turn it out immediately and allow it to dry for 30 minutes. The smaller the bell, the quicker the sugar will dry.

2 Gently lift the sugar bell in your left hand and, using a small spoon, hollow out the inside of the bell. If you wish, return the bell to the mould while you hollow it out. Set the bell aside carefully to dry thoroughly.

3 Pipe a little royal icing inside the bell and attach a silver ball for a clapper.

> NOTE: Children's sand moulds can be used very successfully in sugar moulding as can other hollow objects around the house.

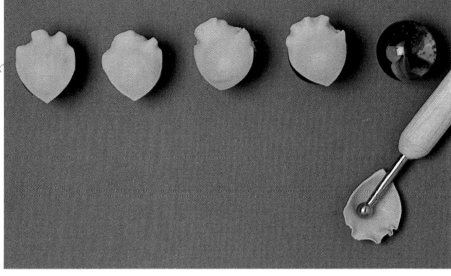

MOULDED FLOWERS

The moulded flowers shown here are used on the cakes in this book or given as alternatives. Moulding flowers is a technique that produces beautiful and realistic results. The ideal way to achieve perfection, however, is to work from nature.

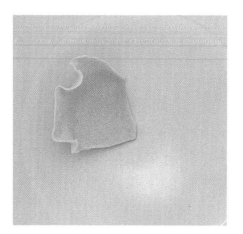

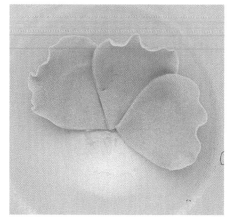

Briar Rose and Leaf

Equipment
pale pink, yellow and green modelling paste
(page 12)
pattern for rose petals and leaves (page 68)
painting knife
medium ball tool
marbles
vegetable fat
stamens
hollow mould
egg white
leaf veiner

1 Roll out the modelling paste thinly and cut out five rose petals.

2 Pick up a petal with a painting knife and place it on to the heel of your hand with the rounded part of the petal away from your palm. Cover the remaining petals with thin plastic.

3 With a medium ball tool, press firmly around the edge of the petal to thin and flute it slightly. Lift the petal and place it in the centre of your palm.

4 Use the ball tool gently to work the centre of the petal to hollow it. Place the petal over a marble to set. Repeat the procedure on the next four petals. Do not let the petals dry completely otherwise assembly will be difficult.

5 Cut 10 mm (½ inch) off each end of a number of stamens. Press a piece of yellow modelling paste the size of half a pea against a piece of tulle or net. Push the stamens into the yellow centre all around the edge and curl the stamens slightly.

6 Put a little vegetable fat in the centre of a hollow mould. Take the first petal, which should still be pliable, and paint egg white on the right-hand straight edge of the petal. Place this petal on the fat in the hollow of the mould. Repeat the procedure with the next four petals, overlapping them by about 5 mm (¼ inch) and lifting the first petal over the last.

7 Paint a little egg white into the centre of the petals and attach the yellow centre with the stamens.

NOTE: *You may find the modelling paste sticking to your hands and fingers if they get too hot. If you have this problem, either dust your hands very lightly with cornflour, or use a little vegetable fat. It is important to use only a little cornflour or it will spoil the look of the petals.*

Leaf
Roll out green modelling paste thinly and cut out the leaves. Vein the leaves with a plastic or rubber veiner. Pinch the leaves very lightly at their base and place them on a curved shape to dry. Never let leaves dry absolutely flat otherwise they look too stiff in an arrangement.

Rose and Bud

Equipment
florist wire
florist tape
pale pink, pale and dark green modelling paste
(page 13)
patterns for calyx and rose petals (page 68)
egg white
ball tool
small scissors

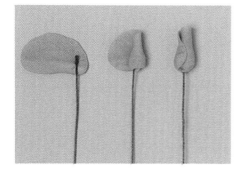

1 Cut green florist tape into four, cover a piece of florist wire and bend over one end. Roll pale pink modelling paste, the size of a large pea, into a ball. Roll into a 'sausage' and then flatten along the length of this roll, flattening one side only.

2 Dip the curved end of the covered florist wire into egg white and place it into one end of the modelling paste. Roll the modelling paste against itself to make a centre for the rose. Set aside to dry.

3 Add the calyx at this stage to form a rosebud. *If a half rose is desired, continue from Step 9 for instructions on how to mould the petals.* Colour modelling paste green and add a touch of brown. Now take a small portion of this paste and add white to it to form a very pale green. Roll out each shade separately, then place one on top of the other, attaching the two layers with egg white if necessary.

4 Roll out the two layers together and cut out the calyx using a calyx cutter or a calyx pattern. Lift the calyx with a painting knife and place it, dark side up, on to the palm of your hand.

5 Move the small end of a ball tool along the length of each sepal and then hollow out the centre of the calyx. Pinch the ends of each sepal to make a point. With small scissors cut a tiny strip away from the base of each sepal.

6 Turn the calyx over and paint egg white on its centre and a little way along each sepal.

7 Join the calyx to the rose by pushing the wire stem through the centre of the calyx. The light side goes against the rose.

8 Roll a piece of darker green paste into a ball the size of a small pea. Flatten one side slightly, paint the flattened side with egg white and push the wire stem through the ball, flat side uppermost, to form the hip of the rose.

9 Roll out pink modelling paste and cut out three smaller rose petals with a petal cutter or use a pattern and a sharp knife. Place a petal in the palm of your hand; hollow and flute it with a ball tool.

10 Paint the base of each petal with egg

white and attach each to the cone, curving the edges outward. Set aside to dry. Following Steps 3–8 above, add the calyx at this stage to form a half rose.

11 For a fuller rose, cut out five larger petals and hollow and flute the petals with a ball tool in the palm of your hand. Paint with egg white and attach to the cone with the three petals attached. Add the calyx, following Steps 3–8 above, and gently curve back the sepals of the calyx.

Hyacinths and Filler Flowers

All bell-shaped flowers are made in the same way, although the number of petals will vary.

Equipment
modelling paste (page 13)
paintbrush
flower cutter
auger tool
covered florist wire
egg white

1 Use a piece of modelling paste the size of a pea and roll it into a ball. Shape it into a 'hat shape' with your fingers, then place the wide part on a board and thin the paste using the handle of a paintbrush.

2 Place a flower cutter over the long centre part and cut out the desired shape. Turn the flower over and hollow the inside with an auger tool.

3 Mark each petal with a pin by making a line along its length. Bend over the end of a piece of covered florist wire, dip it into egg white and thread it through the flower. This will enable you to wire small flowers together in sprays. Stamens may be added if desired.

Forget-me-nots

Equipment
modelling paste (page 13)
flower cutter
ball tool
stamens or thin covered fuse wire
egg white

1 Roll out the modelling paste and cut out the flowers with a flower cutter.

2 Hollow each flower slightly with a ball tool.

3 Dip the stamen, or thin covered fuse wire, into egg white and insert it into the centre of the flower.

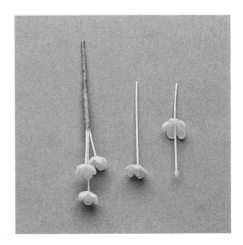

Carnation

Equipment
modelling paste (page 13)
icing knife
auger tool
egg white
covered florist wire
green florist tape
paintbrush
food colouring
white stamens

1 To make a small flower, roll out the modelling paste thinly and cut out a scalloped round about 50 mm (2 inches) in diameter. Using an icing knife, hobby knife or small scissors, cut tiny cuts into the paste all round the edge.

2 Frill the edge of the circle with an auger tool. Paint a cross on the modelling paste with egg white and pinch the centre of the circle from underneath to form a point, making sure that the edges do not stick to one another. Open up the flower with your auger tool to give it a 'fluffy' appearance.

3 Push a piece of covered florist wire, with a looped end, through the flower and allow it to dry. When dry, you may tape a piece of green florist tape around the base.

4 To make a large flower, repeat Steps 1 and 2 above three or four times and then join the parts together with egg white, pressing them together to form a large carnation. (Touch the edges of the petals with a paintbrush dipped in red or pink food colouring, if desired.)

5 Hollow out a ball of green modelling paste, half the size of a marble, into a cup shape. Thin the edge with your fingers and then cut it into five equal sections. Cut each section into a pointed shape. Thread a piece of covered florist wire, with a closed hook

at one end, through the calyx and then stick a small ball of green paste on top of the wire inside the calyx to secure it. Paint the inside of the calyx with egg white. Attach the calyx to the flower by inserting the completed flower into the hollowed calyx.

6 Cut three lengths of white stamen 'stalks' and curl one end of each by scraping the blade of a pair of scissors along it. Dip the straight ends of these stamens into egg white and then insert them into the centre of the carnation.

Pansy

Equipment
modelling paste (page 13)
auger tool
covered florist wire
egg white
flower pattern (page 68)
ball tool
paintbrush
food colouring
royal icing
small writing tube

1 Form the calyx first by rolling a piece of green modelling paste, the size of a large pea, into a ball.

2 Hollow out the ball with an auger tool or thick knitting needle, then thin it by pressing it between your thumb and middle finger.

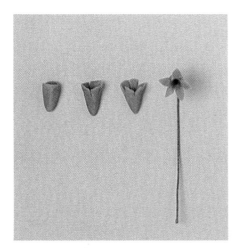

3 Cut the edges of this cup-shape into five and cut each piece into a sharp petal shape. Dip a piece of covered florist wire, bent into a closed hook at one end, into egg white and slip it through the calyx. Curve the wire slightly at the calyx. Allow this to dry thoroughly.

> *NOTE: When making pansies, it is a good idea to make the calyxes well in advance.*

4 Decide on the colour of your pansy, and roll out the modelling paste thinly.

5 Cut out five petals as per the pattern given – two of Shape A, two of Shape B and one of Shape C. Mark with veins by pressing them between your palms.

6 Flute the round edges of each petal slightly with a ball tool, then put them aside to set. Stick the petals, which should still be pliable, into the calyx with egg white. First the top two petals (Shape A) of the pansy, the left one slightly overlapping the right one.

7 Now add the next two matching petals (Shape B) just over the lower edges of the first two. Lastly, attach the single petal (Shape C) to the calyx so that it just touches the last two petals. Set aside to dry, propping up the petals with sponge or cotton wool if necessary.

8 When all five petals are dry, paint the centre of the pansy with violet to which a little red has been added.

9 Paint the two smaller petals from the narrow part to about the halfway mark with the same colour. With white royal icing in a small writing tube, pipe a small crescent shape on the lower edge of the centre opening and then an inverted 'V' at the top of the opening. When this is dry, paint the crescent shape a deep yellow.

Large Daisy

Equipment
modelling clay★
modelling paste (page 13)
covered florist wire
8-petal daisy cutter or pattern (page 69)
ball tool
pin
tulle

1 If possible, make a mould of the base of a real daisy from modelling clay and bake it according to the directions on the packet until it is hard.

2 Push a piece of green modelling paste, the size of a pea, into the mould. Insert a piece of covered wire, with one end bent over, into the modelling paste. Remove the base from the mould and set it aside to dry.

3 Roll out the modelling paste and cut out two daisies with the daisy cutter.

4 Widen each petal slightly by running a small ball tool gently along each petal.

5 Mark lines along the petals with a pin and hollow the centre of each daisy shape with a ball tool.

6 Wet the centre of one daisy and place the other on top, so positioning the upper petals that they cover the spaces below.

7 Press a small ball of deep golden yellow modelling paste against a piece of tulle to mark it.

8 Wet the inside of the green daisy base made in Step 2 and attach the daisy to it.

9 Attach the centre to the flower and place the daisy on a flower stand to dry.

Half-open flowers

1 Roll out yellow modelling paste and cut out one daisy with an 8-petal daisy cutter.

2 Widen each petal slightly by running a small ball tool along its length.

3 Mark lines along the petals with a pin.

4 Pinch the centre and set aside while making the green base. Immediately insert the petals into the green base, pressing the base around the petals.

Bud

1 Make a mould of the base of a daisy from modelling clay. Bake until hard. Push a piece of green modelling paste, the size of a pea, into the mould. Insert a piece of covered wire, with one end bent over, into the modelling paste. Remove the paste from the mould, mark with lines and round the top of the base slightly to form a bud.

Leaf

1 Press a real daisy leaf on to modelling clay and bake it according to the directions on the packet until it is hard.

2 Roll out green modelling paste and cut out the daisy leaves, pressing each one on to the mould to vein it. Set the leaves aside to dry slightly curved.

NOTE: *Modelling clay is available from craft shops.*

Mock Orange Blossom

Equipment
white sewing cotton
tinned copper fuse wire
yellow and green liquid food colourings
white and green modelling paste
(page 13) • florist tape
small daphne cutter
petal cutter or pattern (page 68)

1 Roll the white cotton loosely around your forefinger to a thickness of about 2.5 mm (⅛ inch).

2 Cut a length of fuse wire and slip it through the looped cotton to secure. Twist the wire tightly to hold the cotton firmly. Cut through the cotton on one side.

3 Dip the ends of the cut cotton into yellow food colouring and set aside.

4 Mix together some white and green modelling paste to make a very, very pale green. Roll a miniature sausage of this paste to form the pistil of the flower. Moisten the end of a piece of fuse wire, insert it into the sausage and leave to dry.

5 Tape the pistil and stamens together with florist tape.

6 Using a small daphne cutter, make a green calyx by following the steps for filler flowers (page 34). Insert the wire with stamens and pistil, moisten with water in order to attach and leave to dry.

7 Roll out some white modelling paste and, using a petal cutter or the pattern, cut out four petals. Frill the round edges very slightly and then hollow the petals.

8 Moisten the inside of the calyx with water, attach the petals and leave to dry.

Mimosa

Equipment
covered fuse wire
yellow modelling paste (page 13)
small container of water
paper towels
granulated sugar

1 Bend over one end of the taped wire.

2 Roll a tiny ball of modelling paste. Dip the bent end of the wire in water and then insert the wire in the modelling paste ball. Neaten and set aside to dry.

3 Dip the little modelling paste ball on wire in water, gently dab it on a paper towel and then dip it in the sugar. Leave to dry.

Cymbidium Orchid

Equipment
modelling paste (page 13)
curved modelling tool
dusting powder
paintbrush
food colourings
auger tool
flower cutter or pattern (page 69)
ball tool
orchid former
water
leaf veiner
hollow mould

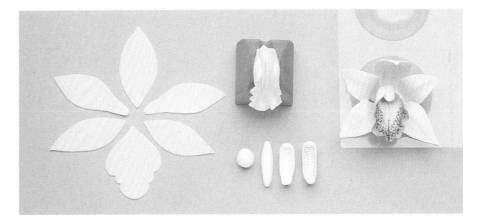

1 Roll a small piece of white modelling paste, about twice the size of a large pea, into a cylinder about 20 mm (¾ inch) long with rounded ends. Using a curved modelling tool, or the back of a paintbrush, press a hollow into its length and then curve the cylinder slightly. Brush with dusting powder to match the shade of the petals. Paint tiny dots of food colouring on the inside curve and set aside to dry.

2 Roll out some modelling paste in the colour of your choice to form the trumpet or lip of the orchid. Leave the paste slightly thicker where the rounded part of the lip will be when it is cut. Using the patterns, cut out the trumpet and flute along the centre curved portion using an auger tool, then hollow the side sections slightly with a ball tool. Place the trumpet or lip on an orchid former to dry in the required shape, pulling the centre section downwards. Colour the trumpet or lip with dusting powder if desired.

3 With yellow modelling paste, roll two very thin cylinders about 2.5 mm (⅛ inch) thick and 10 mm (½ inch) long, each one tapering to a point. Attach the cylinders to the trumpet or lip with a little water.

4 Cut out five petals from the same colour modelling paste used for the trumpet, using a flower cutter or the pattern. Use a leaf veiner to mark the petals with fine lines. Run a ball tool along the edges of each one to refine them. Colour the petals with dusting powder if wished, then place the petals over a curved shape.

5 Grease a hollow mould and add a ball of paste the size of a large pea. Flatten it, paint it with water and then attach the petals and trumpet to create an orchid as shown.

Daisies

Equipment
modelling paste (page 13)
food colourings
daisy cutter or pattern (page 69)
large pin
flower stand
small piece of tulle
covered fuse wire
leaf cutter
fresh leaf or leaf veiner

1 Roll out some modelling paste in the colour of your choice and cut out the daisies, using a daisy cutter or the pattern.

2 Use the large pin to mark the lines on each petal, as shown. Attach two daisies to each other with water and place on a flower stand to set.

3 Roll a small ball of yellow modelling paste and press it against a piece of tulle to mark.

4 Attach the marked, flattened balls to the centre of each daisy with a little water and set aside to dry.

5 For the stems, use a piece of taped fuse wire. Bend the end of the wire and dip it into water. Roll a ball of green modelling paste and mould it to a cone shape, then flatten the top and thread the wire through. Leave to dry.

6 Attach the daisies to the stems with a little water or royal icing.

7 Roll out some pale green modelling paste and cut out the leaves, using a leaf cutter.

8 Vein the leaves, using a fresh leaf or a rubber veiner.

9 Moisten the back of the leaves, attach fuse wire stems. Shape to give a natural appearance and leave to dry.

The Bride and Groom

To bring your talents to the fore, attempt this three-tier cake with its lace pieces, extension work, embroidery and moulded figures.

Ingredients
1 × 150 mm (6 inch) square cake
1 × 225 mm (9 inch) square cake
1 × 300 mm (12 inch) square cake
4 kg (8 lb) white sugarpaste (page 12)
white, red and black modelling paste (page 13)
white and green royal icing (page 12)
flesh-coloured figure moulding paste (page 13)

Materials and Decorations
1 × 200 mm (8 inch) cake board
1 × 275 mm (11 inch) cake board
1 × 375 mm (15 inch) cake board
pink-tinted blossoms and buds (page 64)
pink dusting powder
burgundy hyacinths (page 34)
5 × silver ribbon bows
shell border (page 17)
tubes: Nos. 0, 1, 2 and 3
patterns for embroidery (page 70), lace pieces
(page 71), bride's and groom's clothing
(page 77) • waxed paper
8 × 100 mm (4 inch) pillars or 2 acrylic stands
male and female plastic figure moulds
cocktail sticks
covered wire
auger tool
tulle
2 thin skewers
tiny bouquet of flowers

1 Cover the cakes with white sugarpaste and prepare the bottom and middle tier to accommodate the pillars or acrylic stands by following the instructions on page 15.

2 Make the blossoms and buds with white modelling paste according to the instructions on page 64 (Steps 4 to 7) and brush the centres of the flowers with pink dusting powder.

3 Make the hyacinths from burgundy modelling paste according to the instructions on page 34.

4 Combine the blossoms, buds and hyacinths with the ribbon bows to form five sprays.

5 Pipe a shell border around the base of each cake with white royal icing in a No. 2 writing tube.

6 Select an embroidery design from page 70 and make either a glass stencil (page 24) of the design or pipe the design directly on to the cakes with a No. 0 writing tube and white royal icing.

7 Following the instructions on page 22, pipe the extension work on to each cake with royal icing in a No. 3 writing tube.

8 Pipe the lace pieces of your choice on to waxed paper with a No. 1 writing tube and allow them to dry.

9 Attach the lace pieces to all three cakes.

10 Attach the flower sprays to the cake with a little royal icing.

11 Position the pillars or acrylic stands on the cakes and balance the tiers on them.

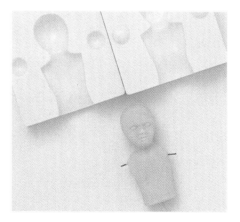

12 Roll pieces of flesh-coloured figure moulding paste into two 'sausages' and thin them, a quarter of the way down where the neck will be, by rolling them between your fingers. Press this paste into the face half of each mould, pressing firmly to ensure clear features.

13 Flatten another two pieces of paste and press them into the torso half of each mould. Press the second half of each mould firmly on to the first to form the head and torso for the bride and groom. Trim away any excess paste and smooth the joins. Remove from the mould and insert half a cocktail stick into each torso and a short piece of covered wire through the shoulders. Allow to dry thoroughly.

14 Brush the cheeks lightly with pale pink dusting powder. Paint the eyes with white water-soluble food colouring, completing the eye by painting with brown food colouring. Paint the bride's mouth with pink food colouring and the groom's with pink mixed with a touch of brown food colouring. Pipe on the hair with royal icing in a No. 1 or 2 writing tube.

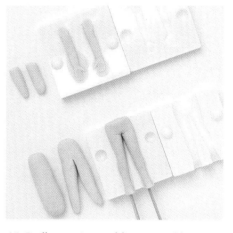

15 Roll two pieces of figure moulding paste into two 'sausages' and then cut them in half as shown. Press the paste into each leg mould and press the second half of the mould firmly on top. Trim away any excess paste and insert a thin skewer into each leg. Immediately attach the torso to the legs by inserting the cocktail stick into the waist. Allow to dry thoroughly.

16 Roll four pieces of flesh-coloured moulding paste into 'sausages' and press each one into an arm mould. Trim away any excess paste and curve the arms as necessary. Press a small hole into each arm to accommodate the wire in the shoulders. Set aside to dry thoroughly.

17 Roll out white modelling paste and cut out the bride's clothing, using the patterns on page 77 as a guide. Cover the pieces with plastic to prevent them drying out. Cut out a 140 mm (5½ inch), 75 mm (3 inch) and 40 mm (1¾ inch) diameter circle from modelling paste. Cut out a 25 mm (1 inch) circle from the middle of the larger and medium circles and a 10 mm (½ inch) circle from the small circle. Frill the edges of each circle slightly with an auger tool.

18 Attach the bodice to the bride by moistening the back and lower edges, then attach the large and medium circle with water or royal icing to form the skirt. Pipe a tiny embroidery design on to the skirt.

19 Attach the sleeves to the arms by moistening all the edges, except the wrists, with water. Cut two small narrow strips from modelling paste, frill them slightly and attach one to each wrist. Attach the arms to the shoulders with royal icing or water. Slit the smaller circle from the outer edge to the centre and attach it to the bodice to form a cape. Gather a piece of tulle and attach it to the head with royal icing to form the veil. Attach a bouquet of tiny flowers to the bride's hands with royal icing.

20 Roll out white, red and black modelling paste and cut out the groom's clothing, using the patterns on page 77 as a guide. Moisten the back and lower edges of the shirt front and attach it to the torso. Attach the shoes to the feet.

21 Form the red modelling paste into a bow tie and attach it to the groom's neck. Attach each trouser leg as shown by moistening the edges. Press a crease into the front of each trouser leg. Attach the jacket and fold over the lapels. Moisten all the edges of the sleeves, except the cuffs, and attach them to the arms. Add a cuff to each wrist and attach the arms to the shoulders with royal icing or water.

22 Position the bride and groom on the top tier, attaching them by pushing the skewers into the cake.

His and Hers

A top hat and picture hat provide a witty alternative to the traditional wedding cake.

Ingredients
2 × 150 mm (6 inch) round cakes
1 × 200 mm (8 inch) round cake
1 kg (2 lb) white sugarpaste (page 12)
1 kg (2 lb) grey sugarpaste (page 12)
500 g (1 lb) white modelling paste (page 13)
grey food colouring
white and grey royal icing (page 12)

Materials and Decorations
1 × 250 mm (10 inch) round cake board
1 × 400 mm (16 inch) round cake board
piece of sponge
1 × 175 mm (7 inch) diameter paper circle
marked into 4
1 × 400 mm (16 inch) diameter paper circle
marked into 4
1 × 250 mm (10 inch) diameter paper circle
marked into 4
tubes: Nos. 1 and 2
7 thin cardboard cones, to support the
brim of the picture hat
pattern for eyelet embroidery (page 71)
39 small mimosa flowers, taped in
groups of 3 (page 38)
8 small white daisies (page 39)
9 medium-sized yellow daisies (page 39)
9 medium-sized apricot daisies (page 39)
5 mm (¼ inch) wide yellow and apricot ribbons
1 × 200 mm (8 inch) high acrylic cutaway stand
1 × 50 mm (2 inch) high acrylic cutaway stand

Top Hat

1 Mix together 250 g (8 oz) of the white sugarpaste and 250 g (8 oz) of the white modelling paste and colour to match the grey sugarpaste.

2 Roll out this mixture and cut out a 250 mm (10 inch) circle. Place the circle on the 250 mm (10 inch) round board and prop up with a piece of sponge to shape.

3 Place the two 150 mm (6 inch) round cakes on top of each other. Fill in any gaps between the cakes with marzipan and spread with sieved apricot jam.

4 Roll out a grey sugarpaste rectangle of 150 × 500 mm (6 × 20 inches). Place the joined cakes on their side and roll the sugarpaste around them, smoothing carefully.

5 Roll out the grey sugarpaste and cut out a 175 mm (7 inch) diameter circle for the top of the hat. Attach and smooth by rubbing gently with your hand.

6 Place the cakes on the shaped circle/hat brim.

7 Cut two lengths of apricot and one length of yellow ribbon to go around the hat and secure them with dots of royal icing.

8 Using a No. 2 tube and grey royal icing, pipe a snail's trail around the crown and edge of brim.

Picture Hat

1 Mix together 250 g (8 oz) white modelling paste and 500 g (1 lb) white sugarpaste and set aside for the brim of the hat.

2 Centre the 200 mm (8 inch) round cake on the large cake board and cover with white sugarpaste.

3 Roll out the white modelling paste and sugarpaste mixture, rolling it more thinly towards the outer edge.

4 Cut out a 400 mm (16 inch) diameter circle from this mixture and mark the centre. Cut out a 175 mm (7 inch) diameter circle from the centre of the circle.

5 Lift the outer circle over the cake and down on to the cake board.

6 Lift the circle at intervals to create the brim, supporting it with cardboard cones.

7 Immediately cut out the eyelet embroidery design around the brim, using the pattern. Using a No. 1 tube and white royal icing, pipe around each opening. Embroider dots and leaves between the openings, as shown in the photograph.

8 Position some of the daisies against the hat while they are still damp, fitting them snugly against the hat and brim.

9 Arrange the remaining daisies and the mimosa sprays around brim of the hat, attaching them with royal icing.

10 Trim the edge of the brim with a picot edge made from white royal icing, following the instructions on page 21, using a No. 2 tube for the first row of dots and a No. 1 tube for subsequent rows.

11 Add a ribbon bow and two lengths of ribbon at the back of the hat.

12 Position the cakes on the stands.

Ornamental Orchids

The pale pink sides visible beneath the extension work, make this an attractive and delicate-looking cake.

Ingredients
1 × 300 mm (12 inch) hexagonal cake
1 × 200 mm (8 inch) hexagonal cake
pink and white modelling paste (page 13)
3 kg (6 lb) white sugarpaste (page 12)
white royal icing (page 12)

Materials and Decorations
1 × 375 mm (15 inch) hexagonal cake board
1 × 250 mm (10 inch) hexagonal cake board
patterns for cymbidium orchid petals (page 69),
embroidery designs (page 70),
lace pieces (page 71)
cymbidium orchids (page 39)
pink dusting powder
pink and white hyacinths (page 34)
cornflour
shell border (page 17)
waxed paper
tubes: Nos. 0, 1 and 2
silver ribbon bows (page 29)
4 × 100 mm (4 inch) pillars or an acrylic stand

1 Mould the orchids from white modelling paste as directed on page 39. Paint the tongue with pink dusting powder.

2 Mould hyacinths and buds from pink and white modelling paste following the instructions on page 34.

3 Place the cakes on cake boards and cover the cakes with white sugarpaste. Prepare the bottom tier to accommodate the pillars or acrylic stand by following the instructions on page 15.

4 Select an embroidery design from page 70 and make either a glass stencil of the design or pipe it directly on to the cake, using a No. 1 writing tube.

5 Mix pink dusting powder with a little cornflour to create a pale shade and brush the lower part of the cake sides beneath the embroidery design.

6 Pipe a shell border around the base of each cake with white royal icing in a No. 2 writing tube.

7 Execute the extension work as described on page 22. Using a No. 0 or 1 writing tube, pipe the lace pieces on to waxed paper as described on page 21.

8 Arrange the orchids, hyacinths and ribbon bows into sprays and position them on the top and bottom tiers.

9 Pipe small dots in 25 mm (1 inch) sections with a small writing tube and attach the lace pieces.

10 Position the pillars or acrylic stand on the bottom tier and balance the other tier on top.

Lyre and Cupids

Delicately beautiful in pastel shades, this wedding cake features a romantic theme of cupids and flowers.

Ingredients
1 × 300 mm (12 inch) square cake
1 × 200 mm (8 inch) square cake
3 kg (6 lb) pale pink sugarpaste (page 12)
white pastillage (page 13)
white and pale pink royal icing (page 12)
white, pale and darker pink, blue and yellow modelling paste (page 13)

Materials and Decorations
1 × 350 mm (14 inch) square cake board
1 × 250 mm (10 inch) square cake board
silver braid
glue
pattern for lyre (page 74), lace pieces (page 71)
gold sewing thread for strings of lyre
tubes: Nos. 1 and 2
non-toxic gold powder
gin, vodka or caramel oil flavouring
fine paintbrush
plastic cupid mould
cornflour
pin
waxed paper
pink roses and buds (page 33)
pink dusting powder
white daisies (page 37)
blue bell-shaped flowers (page 34)
florist tape
cotton wool
pink ribbon bows
shell border (page 17)
100 mm (4 inch) pillars or an acrylic stand

1 Cut off the corners of the cakes and the cake boards to create the octagonal shape. Glue fancy silver braid around the edges of the boards.

2 Cover the cakes with pale pink sugarpaste, preparing the bottom tier to accommodate the stand or pillars by following the instructions on page 15.

3 Roll out the pastillage to about 2.5 mm (⅛ inch) thick and cut out two lyres, using either the pattern or a lyre cutter.

4 Attach the strings to one cross bar and to one half of the lyre with royal icing. Sandwich the lyre together by placing the second cross bar and other half of the lyre on top.

5 Pipe beading around the lyre with royal icing in a No. 1 writing tube and allow to dry thoroughly.

6 Mix the gold powder with a little gin, vodka or caramel oil flavouring and paint the beading, and strings if necessary, using a very fine paintbrush.

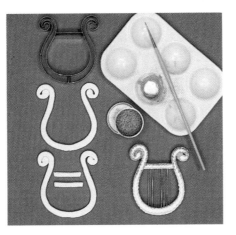

7 Make eight cupids by placing white modelling paste or sugarpaste into a cupid mould after first lightly dusting the modelling paste or sugarpaste with cornflour. Remove the cupids with a pin and allow them to dry thoroughly.

8 Select a lace piece design on page 71 and pipe the pieces on to waxed paper, following the instructions on page 21, and allow them to dry thoroughly.

9 Mould pale pink roses and darker pink buds from modelling paste, following the instructions on page 33. Brush pink dusting powder into the centre of each rose.

10 Mould the daisies from white modelling paste following the instructions on page 39.

11 Mould small blue bell-shaped flowers, following the instructions for hyacinths on page 34.

12 Tape the roses, rosebuds and bell-shaped flowers into eight crescent-shaped sprays and attach them to the sides of both cakes with royal icing.

13 Attach the lyre to the top of the cake with royal icing, supporting the lyre with cotton wool until the icing has set.

14 Paint the lyres held by the cupids with gold and attach the cupids to the sides of the cake with royal icing.

15 Attach a spray of roses, rosebuds, daisies and bell-shaped flowers to the top of the cake together with pink ribbon bows.

16 Pipe a shell border around the base of each cake with pale pink royal icing in a No. 2 writing tube. Pipe a 25 mm (1 inch) row of dots with white royal icing and attach the lace pieces at an angle to each cake. Position the pillars or acrylic stand and balance the other tier on top.

Orange Blossoms

The pale green icing and dainty orange blossoms make this an unusual wedding cake.

Ingredients
1 × 200 mm (8 inch) hexagonal cake
1 × 300 mm (12 inch) hexagonal cake
white modelling paste (page 13)
3 kg (6 lb) pale green sugarpaste (page 12)
white, green and yellow royal icing (page 12)

Materials and decorations
1 × 250 mm (10 inch) hexagonal cake board
1 × 350 mm (14 inch) hexagonal cake board
patterns for hearts (page 72), orange blossoms
(page 68), lace pieces (page 71)
waxed paper
tubes: Nos. 0 and 2
flower cutter
auger tool
pale yellow dusting powder
stamens
florist wire
yellow ribbon bows
snail's trail (page 16)
4 × 100 mm (4 inch) pillars or an acrylic stand

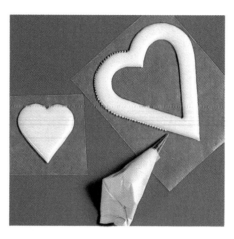

1 Flood the large heart (Shape C) and six smaller hearts (Shape B) on waxed paper with white royal icing according to the instructions on page 19 and allow them to dry.

2 Before removing the hearts from the waxed paper, pipe tiny yellow dots along the edges with royal icing in a No. 0 writing tube.

3 Make the orange blossoms by moulding a 'hat-shape' with white modelling paste and cutting the edges with a flower cutter. Hollow the flowers slightly with an auger tool and dust the centre of each flower with pale yellow dusting powder.

4 Cut off the ends of the stamens and use only the 'stalks'. Wet the ends of the 'stalks' and insert them into the flower.

5 Roll white modelling paste into oval shapes to form the buds and attach them to pieces of florist wire.

6 Arrange the flowers, buds and yellow ribbon bows into six sprays.

7 Pipe the lace designs on to waxed paper and leave them to dry.

8 Cover the cakes with pale green sugarpaste and prepare the bottom tier to accommodate the pillars or acrylic stand by following the instructions on page 15.

9 Pipe a snail's trail around the base of each cake with green royal icing in a No. 2 writing tube.

10 Attach a small ball of white sugarpaste to the centre of the top tier with a little royal icing and insert the point of the large heart into the sugarpaste. Support the heart until the icing is dry.

11 Arrange the remaining orange blossoms, buds and ribbon bows into a posy around the large heart.

12 Attach two orange blossoms to the large heart with a little royal icing.

13 Attach the flower sprays and small hearts to the sides of the cakes with royal icing.

14 Attach the lace pieces at an angle all around the base of each tier.

15 Position the pillars or acrylic stand on the bottom tier and balance the other tier on top.

A Basket of Roses

This cake, with its flower-filled basket, lace and extension work, is fit for any bride.

Ingredients

1 × 200 mm (8 inch) oval cake
1 × 300 mm (12 inch) oval cake
white pastillage (page 13)
white royal icing (page 12)
3 kg (6 lb) white sugarpaste (page 12)
green, pink, blue and white modelling paste
(page 13)

Materials and decorations

1 × 250 mm (10 inch) oval cake board
1 × 375 mm (15 inch) oval cake board
plastic bell for mould
cornflour
patterns for basket (page 72),
lace pieces (page 71)
roses (page 33)
white hyacinths (page 34)
blue forget-me-nots (page 34)
shell border (page 17)
tubes: Nos. 2 and 42
waxed paper
pink and white ribbon bows (page 29)
4 × 100 mm (4 inch) white pillars or
an acrylic stand

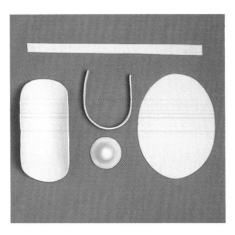

1 Make the stand for the basket by rolling out white pastillage and cutting a circle large enough to go over the plastic bell. Lightly dust the bell with cornflour and press the pastillage firmly over the bell. Move it around every few minutes to prevent the pastillage from sticking to the bell. Remove the pastillage when it can hold its shape.

2 Using the pattern on page 72, cut out an oval for the basket out of white pastillage. Leave to dry in a slightly curved shape.

3 Cut out a 10 × 225 mm (1 × 9 inch) wide strip of pastillage for the handle and allow it to set in a curve to fit the oval base.

4 When all the pieces are dry, attach the curved oval to the bell-shaped base with royal icing and allow it to dry.

5 Attach the handle to the basket with royal icing and support it until it is completely dry.

6 Make the roses, hyacinths and forget-me-nots according to the instructions on pages 33 and 34 and when they are dry, fill the basket with the flowers by pushing them into a small piece of sugarpaste. Start with the centre flower and those at either end and on each side, then fill in the gaps with the remaining flowers and ribbon bows.

7 Cover the cakes with sugarpaste and position the basket of flowers on the top tier, attaching it with a little royal icing. Edge the base of the basket with small shells using a No. 42 star tube and white royal icing. Prepare the bottom tier to accommodate the pillars or acrylic stand by following the instructions on page 15.

8 Select a lace piece design and pipe the pieces on to waxed paper, following the instructions on page 21 and allow them to dry thoroughly.

9 Pipe a shell border around the base of each cake with white royal icing in a No. 2 writing tube.

10 Pipe the extension work around the lower half of each cake following the instructions on page 22.

11 Make up small sprays of flowers with ribbon bows and attach them to the cakes with royal icing.

12 Attach the lace pieces to the top edge of the extension work by following the instructions on page 21.

13 Position the pillars or acrylic stand on the bottom tier and balance the other tier on top.

Wedding Bell

This lavender-coloured wedding cake incorporates two simple techniques: floodwork and sugar moulding.

Ingredients

1 × 300 × 250 mm (12 × 10 inch) oval cake
royal icing (page 12)
moulding sugar (page 30)
1.5 kg (3 lb) lavender sugarpaste (page 12)
pale pink, lavender and white modelling paste (page 13)

Materials and decorations

1 × 350 × 300 mm (14 × 12 inch) oval cake board
pattern for bell, bride and groom (page 78),
embroidery bell design (page 72),
lace pieces (page 71)
plastic mould for bell
food colouring in assorted colours
paintbrush
piece of glass
tubes: Nos. 0, 1 and 42
ribbon inserter
10 mm (½ inch) wide lavender ribbon
waxed paper
miniature pale pink roses and buds (page 33)
small white and lavender bell-type flowers (page 34)
lavender ribbon bows (page 29)
shell border (page 17)

1 Flood the picture of the bride and groom with royal icing, following the instructions for Floodwork on page 19. Allow the picture to dry.

2 Fill a plastic bell mould with moulding sugar, packing it in firmly and turning it out immediately. If you are unable to obtain the mould, trace the outline given on page 73 and make the bell in modelling paste or sugarpaste, cutting out the inner shape to accommodate the bride and groom. Allow the bell to dry thoroughly.

3 Paint the bride and groom according to the photograph and allow them to dry.

4 Attach the floodwork design to the sugar bell with royal icing and allow to set.

5 Pipe the embroidery design on to a piece of glass with royal icing in a No. 0 writing tube and allow it to dry.

6 Place the cake on the cake board and cover the cake with the lavender sugarpaste.

Immediately press the glass stencil on to the sides of the cake.

7 Cuts slots in the icing with a ribbon inserter, following the instructions for Ribbon insertion on page 30.

8 Cut the lavender ribbon into 30 mm (1¼ inch) lengths and insert them into the slots as shown.

9 Follow the embroidery design with a No. 1 writing tube and white royal icing and allow it to dry.

10 Position the bell on top of the cake, attaching it with royal icing.

11 Pipe the lace pieces on to waxed paper with a No. 0 or 1 writing tube and white royal icing and set them aside to dry.

12 Make up miniature roses and rosebuds from pale pink modelling paste, following the instructions on page 33. Mould small filler flowers from white and lavender modelling paste as described on page 34. Arrange the flowers and lavender ribbon bows into a spray and position it on top of the cake.

13 Trim the bell with royal icing in a No. 1 writing tube and pipe shells (one up and one down) around the base of the cake with a No. 42 star tube.

14 Attach the lace pieces to the cake following the instructions on page 21.

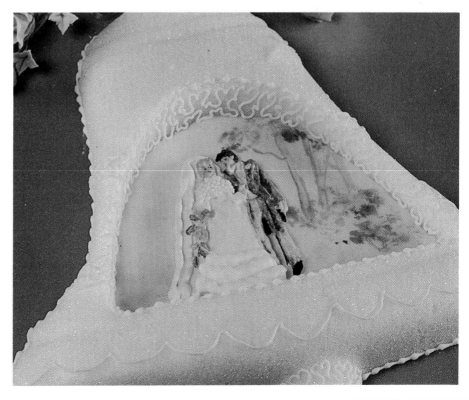

Carnation Cascade

The unusual shape, apricot carnations, cream hyacinths and white forget-me-nots make this an appealing wedding cake.

Ingredients
1 × 200 mm (8 inch) square cake
1 × 300 mm (12 inch) square cake
3 kg (6 lb) white sugarpaste (page 12)
apricot, white and cream modelling paste
(page 13)
white royal icing (page 12)

Materials and decorations
1 × 250 mm (10 inch) cloverleaf cake board
1 × 375 mm (15 inch) cloverleaf cake board
pattern for cloverleaf shape (page 74)
apricot carnations (page 35)
white forget-me-nots (page 34)
cream hyacinths (page 34)
covered florist wire
pull-up shells and loops (page 17)
tubes: Nos. 1 and 8
white ribbon bows (page 29)
4 × 100 mm (4 inch) pillars or an acrylic stand

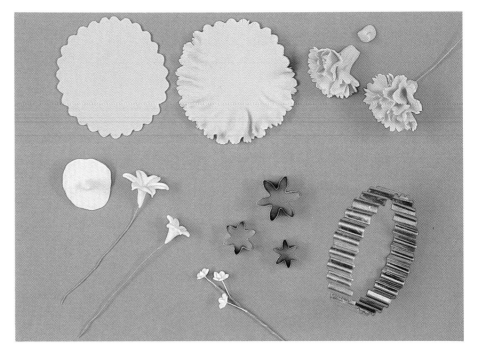

1 Cut each cake into a cloverleaf shape using the pattern on page 74 as a guide.

2 Place the cakes on the cake boards and cover each one with white sugarpaste. Prepare the bottom tier to accommodate the pillars or acrylic stand by following the instructions on page 15.

3 Make the carnations, forget-me-nots and hyacinths by following the instructions on the relevant pages.

4 Pipe pull-up shells around the base of each cake with a No. 8 star tube and white royal icing.

5 Pipe loops with a No. 1 writing tube and white royal icing to complete the cake.

6 Make up 16 small sprays of flowers and ribbon bows and attach them to the sides of both tiers with royal icing.

7 Arrange the flowers on a ball of sugarpaste in the centre of the top tier to form a posy.

8 Position the pillars or acrylic stand on the bottom tier. Make up a larger spray of flowers and ribbon bows and attach it to the centre of the bottom tier with royal icing. Place the smaller tier on top.

Birdbath with Fuchsias

The centre of this unusual cake has been cut out and used as the top tier. The bevel base also adds to the exclusivity of the design.

Ingredients
1 × 150 mm (6 inch) round cake
1 × 300 mm (12 inch) round cake
burgundy, pink and white modelling paste (page 13)
white pastillage (page 13)
white, pale pink and pale green royal icing (page 12)
3 kg (6 lb) white sugarpaste (page 12)

Materials and decorations
1 × 200 mm (8 inch) round cake board
1 × 375 mm (15 inch) round cake board
pattern for birdbath (page 73),
embroidery design (page 70)
biscuit cutter
plastic mould
tubes: Nos. 0, 1, 2, 3 and 42
piece of glass
non-toxic silver powder
little alcohol or caramel oil
1 × 375 mm (15 inch) circle of expanded styrene, 25 mm (1 inch) thick and shaped to give the effect in the picture
shell border (page 17)
white ribbon bows (page 29)
200 mm (8 inch) acrylic stand

1 Prepare the two cake tins for baking.

2 Place the smaller cake tin in the centre of the larger one. Fill both tins with cake mixture and bake as directed on page 11. This is easier than cutting a circle from the centre of the large cake and will prevent rough edges.

3 Make the small fuchsias from pink and burgundy modelling paste and the jasmine from white according to the photographs.

4 Shape white pastillage into a cone shape for the base of the birdbath. Cut out a scalloped circle with a biscuit cutter and place it over a plastic mould to form the bath. Allow both to dry.

5 Use a No. 0 writing tube to pipe Cornelli work (page 16) on the outside of the birdbath, leaving a small circle clear in the centre, and on the cone. Attach the top to the base with royal icing and allow it to set and dry thoroughly.

6 Pipe the embroidery design on to a piece of glass with a No. 0 writing tube and royal icing and allow to dry.

7 Using a No. 1 writing tube and royal icing, pipe the wings and tails of the two small birds as shown and allow them to dry. Assemble the birds by piping the bodies and immediately attaching the wings and tails. When the birds are dry, touch the wings with silver powder mixed with a little alcohol or caramel oil.

8 Stick the bevelled styrene to the larger cake board with royal icing and cover it with sugarpaste.

9 Roll out the icing for the bottom tier into a large circle and cut a cross in the centre. *The icing must be very pliable and thicker in the centre.* Place the icing over the cake, working quickly to get the icing smooth. Trim away the excess icing in the centre.

10 Place the cake on the covered styrene and immediately press the embroidery

design on to the sides of the cake with the glass stencil.

11 Cover the top tier with sugarpaste and immediately press the embroidery design on to the sides.

12 Attach the birdbath to the top tier with royal icing and then add the birds.

13 Pipe the embroidery design with a No. 1 writing tube using pale pink royal icing for the embroidered flowers, pale green for the leaves and white for the birds.

14 Pipe a small shell border, preferably with a No. 42 star tube, around the base of each tier and on the inside lower edge of the bottom tier.

15 Mark the positions for the scallops on the bevel by placing three dots immediately above each other and about 10 mm (½ inch) apart. The first dot must be about 10 mm (½ inch) from the top edge. Do the same on the other side of the bevel immediately opposite the first (i.e. at twelve o'clock and six o'clock) and then at the quarter marks (nine o'clock and three o'clock) and so on until the dots are evenly spaced around the bevel and approximately 25 mm (1 inch) apart.

16 Pipe scallops on the bevel, allowing the loops to fall between every two dots. Start with a No. 3 writing tube and white royal icing for the first row of scallops. Pipe a second line over this row with a No. 2 writing tube. Make a second row of scallops using the same tube. With pink royal icing and a No. 1 writing tube, pipe a row of scallops along the top row of dots and then overline the first and second rows of scallops with this pink as well.

17 Tape the fuchsias and jasmine into a garland and place it on top of the larger cake. Tape the remaining flowers and ribbon into a spray for the top tier.

18 Place acrylic stand in centre of the larger cake and balance the smaller on it.

Fountain Fantasy

Although a spectacular effect is created with the addition of a fountain, this design can also be used as a two-tier cake with pleasing results.

Ingredients
1 × 200 mm (8 inch) round cake
1 × 300 mm (12 inch) round cake
2 kg (4 lb) white sugarpaste (page 12)
white modelling paste (page 13)
white royal icing (page 12)

Materials and decorations
1 × 250 mm (10 inch) round cake board
1 × 350 mm (14 inch) round cake board
1 × 400 mm (16 inch) round cake board
cymbidium orchids (page 39)
pink dusting powder
pink food colouring
paintbrush
white hyacinths (page 34)
cornflour
shell border (page 17)
tube: No. 7
fountain (optional)
4 × 350 mm (14 inch) acrylic stand
pink ribbon bows (page 29)
4 × 150 mm (6 inch) pillars or an acrylic stand

1 Place the cakes on the cake boards and cover the cakes with white sugarpaste. Prepare the bottom tier to accommodate the pillars or acrylic stand by following the instructions on page 15.

2 Make the orchids in white modelling paste, following the instructions on page 39. When dry, shade the tongue (or trumpet) with pink dusting powder and paint on tiny pink dots.

3 Make the hyacinths in white modelling paste according to the instructions on page 34. When the flowers are dry, brush the tips of the petals with pink dusting powder mixed with a little cornflour.

4 Shade the lower half of each cake with pale pink dusting powder and then pipe a shell border around the base of each cake with royal icing and a No. 7 star tube.

5 Place the fountain and the 350 mm (14 inch) acrylic stand on the large cake board.

6 Arrange a wreath of orchids, hyacinths and ribbon bows on the bottom tier. Make a posy of flowers and ribbon bows on the top tier. Place orchids and ribbon bows around the fountain.

7 Balance the bottom tier on the 350 mm (14 inch) acrylic stand and place the 150 mm (6 inch) pillars or acrylic stand in position on the bottom tier, then balance the other tier on top.

Rosebuds and Butterflies

This exquisite cake lends itself to many attractive ideas for table decorations and gifts for guests at a wedding.

Ingredients
1 × 200 mm (8 inch) round cake
1 × 300 mm (12 inch) round cake
3 kg (6 lb) white sugarpaste (page 12)
white pastillage (page 13)
white and pale pink modelling paste (page 13)
white royal icing (page 12)

Materials and decorations
1 × 250 mm (10 inch) round cake board
1 × 350 mm (14 inch) round cake board
1 × 400 mm (16 inch) round cake board
fancy silver edging for boards
snail's trail (page 16)
tubes: Nos. 1 and 3
paper
pin
small white roses (page 33)
pink dusting powder
cornflour
pale pink hyacinths (page 34)
small flower cutter
red-tipped stamens (dip tips of white stamens in red or pink food colouring)
fuse wire
pattern and stencil for butterfly wings (page 73)
thin cardboard
waxed paper
18 fine black stamens for feelers
sponge or cotton wool
plastic mould for shell
straight-edge cutter or hobby knife
4 × 100 mm (4 inch) pillars or an acrylic stand

1 Cover each board with white sugarpaste and cut out a circle the size of each cake from the centre of the two smaller boards. Cut a circle out of the largest board the size of the medium-sized board.

2 Cover the cakes with white sugarpaste and position the cakes on the cake boards and the medium-sized cake board on the largest board. Trim each board with fancy silver edging.

3 Prepare the bottom tier to accommodate the pillars or acrylic stand by following the instructions on page 15. Pipe a snail's trail around the base of each cake with white royal icing in a No. 1 writing tube.

4 Cut out two paper circles 200 mm (8 inch) and 300 mm (12 inch) in diameter respectively. Divide each circle into eight equal parts and mark the eight points around the outer edge of each cake with a pin.

5 Use the two smallest sizes of rose petals and make the roses with white modelling paste, following the instructions on page 33. Brush the centres of the roses with pink dusting powder and the tips with pale pink dusting powder. (Add a little cornflour to make a paler shade.)

6 Make the hyacinths with pale pink modelling paste following the instructions on page 34.

7 Attach a few red-tipped stamens to fuse wire. Using white modelling paste, cut out the blossoms with a flower cutter and hollow them slightly. Brush the blossoms with pink dusting powder (see photograph on page 64 for the Make a Wish cake). Thread the wire through the centre of the flower.

8 Roll out white modelling paste or pastillage very thinly and cut out the butterfly wings to make left and right wings.

9 Cut out a stencil from a thin piece of cardboard. When the wings are dry, place the stencil against each wing and brush dry pink dusting powder on to the exposed part to give it a scalloped edge. Turn the wings over and brush a little pink dusting powder on to the wing where it will meet the body.

10 Pipe the body and head on to a piece of waxed paper with white royal icing in a No. 3 writing tube. Position the wings and the feelers (fine black stamens) into the royal icing while it is still wet. Support the wings with sponge or cotton wool until the body is thoroughly dry.

11 Roll out a piece of white pastillage and place it in a clear plastic mould dusted with cornflour. Keep tipping the pastillage out of the mould so it does not stick. When it has set sufficiently to hold its shape, remove shell from mould and leave to dry.

12 Place a small piece of sugarpaste in the shell and arrange the flowers so that they fill the shell.

13 Roll out white modelling paste very thinly and cut out 5 mm (¼ inch) wide ribbons with a straight-edge cutter or hobby knife. A tracing wheel or comb may be used to edge the ribbon to give a more realistic finish. For the bows, cut a V-shape into each ribbon end.

14 Use two lengths of ribbon and attach two ends to the moulded shell with royal icing. Position the shell on top of the cake, attaching it with royal icing. Raise the ribbons and support them over a piece of sponge or folded cardboard, allowing the loose ends to rest on the cake thus forming a support for the butterfly. When thoroughly dry, attach a butterfly to the ribbon with a little royal icing.

15 Drape lengths of ribbon between the eight marked positions on each cake and allow them to dry. Attach a butterfly to each point on the bottom tier with royal icing.

16 Shape lengths of ribbon into bows and attach them to the top tier at each alternate point marked and around the base of the bottom tier as shown.

17 Arrange the flowers in sprays and attach them to the cakes.

18 Place the pillars or acrylic stand in position and balance the other tier on top.

Horse and Carriage

A romantic means of transport for the bridal couple to use on their wedding day.

Ingredients
250 × 200 mm (10 × 8 inch) oval cake
1 kg (2 lb) pale blue sugarpaste (page 12)
white pastillage or modelling paste 2,
(page 13)
white royal icing (page 12)

Materials and decorations
300 × 250 mm (12 × 10 inch) oval cake board
10 mm (½ inch) half-round crimper
patterns for horse and carriage (page 75)
waxed paper
tubes: Nos. 0, 1 and 2, and small star

1 Cover the cake with pale blue sugarpaste and immediately crimp the top edge using the half-round crimper.

2 Roll out the white pastillage or modelling paste and cut out the horses, using the pattern.

3 Pipe the carriage wheels on to waxed paper using a No. 2 tube and white royal icing for the outlines and a No. 1 tube for the inside spokes and other details. Fill in the centres of the wheels using a No. 1 tube with royal icing which has been softened with a few drops of water.

4 Pipe the carriage outline and scrolls with a No. 1 tube on to waxed paper.

5 Pipe the trellis on the door and the side of the carriage with a No. 0 tube and then overline with a No. 0 tube.

6 The dickey is outlined with a No. 2 tube and the trellis and scrolls are piped with a No. 1 tube.

7 Pipe a mane, tail and harness on one side of each horse using a No. 1 tube.

8 Trace the outline of the carriage on to the cake.

9 Using dots of royal icing, attach the front and back wheels, referring to the photograph for guidance on position.

10 Attach one horse in the correct position, using royal icing.

11 Pipe three lines with a No. 2 tube one on top of the other over the outlines for the carriage and dickey and over the shaft between the horses. Leave to dry.

12 Gently peel the piped carriage off the waxed paper.

13 Pipe an additional line with a No. 2 tube over the carriage outline on the cake and immediately place the piped carriage on top of this line, pressing gently to secure.

14 Repeat Step 13 with the dickey.

15 Pipe a line with a No. 2 tube over the shaft on top of the first horse and attach the second horse on top of this line.

16 Attach the second set of two wheels by building up an axle in royal icing using a No. 2 tube.

17 Overline the crimping with a No. 1 tube.

18 Pipe a dot at each point of the crimping on the top of the cake.

19 Pipe three graduated dots on the side of the cake below the points of the crimping, referring to the photograph for guidance.

20 Using a small star tube, pipe a shell border around the base of the cake.

21 Pipe the reins from the dickey to the horses using a No. 1 tube and white royal icing.

Make a Wish

The combination of yellow and white is used most successfully for this single tier wedding cake.

Ingredients
1 × 250 mm (10 inch) hexagonal cake
white pastillage (page 13)
white, pale green and yellow royal icing
(page 12)
white modelling paste (page 13)
1 kg (2 lb) white sugarpaste (page 12)

Materials and decorations
1 × 325 mm (13 inch) hexagonal cake board
patterns for brick design (page 76),
well (page 76)
tubes: Nos. 1 and 42
piece of glass
cardboard
jar
stamens
fuse wire
florist tape
blossom cutter
ball tool
yellow dusting powder
cornflour
pull-up shells with loops (page 17)
shell border (page 17)
white and yellow ribbon bows (page 29)

1 Pipe the brick design on to glass with royal icing in a No. 1 writing tube, following the instructions for making a glass stencil on page 24. Allow it to dry.

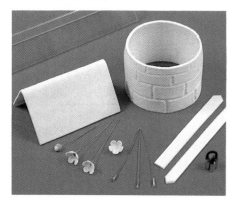

2 Cut out the parts of the wishing well from pastillage, using the patterns on page 76 as a guide. Immediately press the glass stencil against the sides of the well to mark it. Wrap the base of the well around a jar or tin to form the circular shape. Cover a piece of cardboard, shaped to form the roof, with pastillage and allow all the parts to dry thoroughly.

3 When the parts are dry, assemble the well with royal icing.

4 Cut short lengths of stamen 'stems' and 100 mm (4 inch) lengths of fuse wire. Attach the stamens to the fuse wire by twisting one end of the wire around five stamens.

5 Cut florist tape into four and with one strip, tape the length of the wire including the twisted wire attaching the stamens.

6 Roll out white modelling paste and cut out the blossoms with a blossom cutter. Hollow the blossoms with a ball tool and brush the centres with yellow dusting powder toned down with a little cornflour.

7 Push the wire stems through the centres of the flowers and set them aside to dry. Pipe a little green royal icing under the flower to attach it firmly to the stem. Allow to dry thoroughly.

8 Cover the cake with white sugarpaste and pipe pull-up shells with white royal icing and a No. 42 star tube around the base of the cake. Pipe the loops with yellow royal icing in a No. 1 writing tube.

9 Attach the well to the cake with royal icing. Pipe a tiny shell border around the base of the well and on the edge of the roof with white royal icing in a No. 42 star tube.

10 Tape the flowers into a large spray and attach it to the wishing well with a yellow and white ribbon bow.

11 Make up seven small flower sprays with ribbon bows and attach one to each corner of the cake and to one side of the well.

Spring Flowers

With its teardrop-shaped top tier and square bottom tier, this cake is an attractive and pleasing design for a spring wedding.

Ingredients
1 × 225 mm (9 inch) teardrop-shaped cake
1 × 300 mm (12 inch) square cake
3 kg (6 lb) cream sugarpaste (page 12)
orange and yellow royal icing (page 12)
pale lemon, orange and green modelling paste
(page 13)

Materials and decorations
1 × 260 mm (10½ inch) teardrop cake board
1 × 375 mm (15 inch) square cake board
pattern for embroidery design (page 70)
piece of glass
tubes: Nos. 0, 1, 2 and 42
small shell border (page 17)
miniature daffodil cutter (including a small
scalloped cutter)
egg white
covered florist wire
stamens
primrose or primula flower cutter
auger tool
orange dusting powder
small orange bell-shaped flowers (page 34)
bronze and white ribbon bows (page 29)
4 × 100 mm (4 inch) pillars or an acrylic stand

1 Pipe the embroidery design of your choice on to a piece of glass with royal icing in a No. 0 writing tube and allow it to dry.

2 Place the cakes on the cake boards and cover the cakes with cream sugarpaste. Immediately press the glass stencil on to the sides of the cakes. Prepare the bottom tier to accommodate the pillars or acrylic stand by following the instructions on page 15.

3 Using a No. 1 writing tube and royal icing follow the imprint of the embroidery design in yellow and orange.

4 Pipe a small shell border around the base of each cake with a No. 42 star tube and yellow icing.

5 Make the daffodils by moulding yellow modelling paste into a bell-shape and then cutting the edges with the scalloped cutter.

6 Roll out yellow modelling paste and cut out the six-petal shape and attach the scalloped-edge cup to this with egg white or water. Thread a piece of covered wire through both parts, first bending the wire over at one end.

7 Add a few ready-made stamens or pipe some into the cup-shape using a No. 1 writing tube and yellow royal icing.

8 Make the primroses by moulding a small 'Mexican' hat out of pale lemon modelling paste. Cut out the flower with the primula or primrose cutter.

9 Hollow the centre slightly with an auger tool and thread covered wire into the flower. Allow it to dry.

10 Brush the centre of the primrose with orange dusting powder.

11 Make the buds by rolling lemon yellow modelling paste into a ball. Roll out green modelling paste and cut out the calyx. Wrap the calyx around the ball and thread a piece of covered florist wire through the calyx and bud.

12 Use orange modelling paste to mould the bell-shaped flowers, following the instructions for making hyacinths on page 34. Attach the flowers to covered florist wire and set them aside to dry thoroughly.

13 Tape the dry flowers and ribbon bows together into small and large sprays and position them on the cakes as shown.

14 Position the pillars or acrylic stand on the bottom tier and place the other tier on top.

Patterns

Pansy A

Pansy B

Pansy C

Miniature Orchid

Rose Calyx

Rose Leaves

Rose Leaves

Hyacinth

Rose Leaves

Rose Petals

Leaf

Carnation

Carnation

Carnation

Forget-me-nots

Holly Leaves

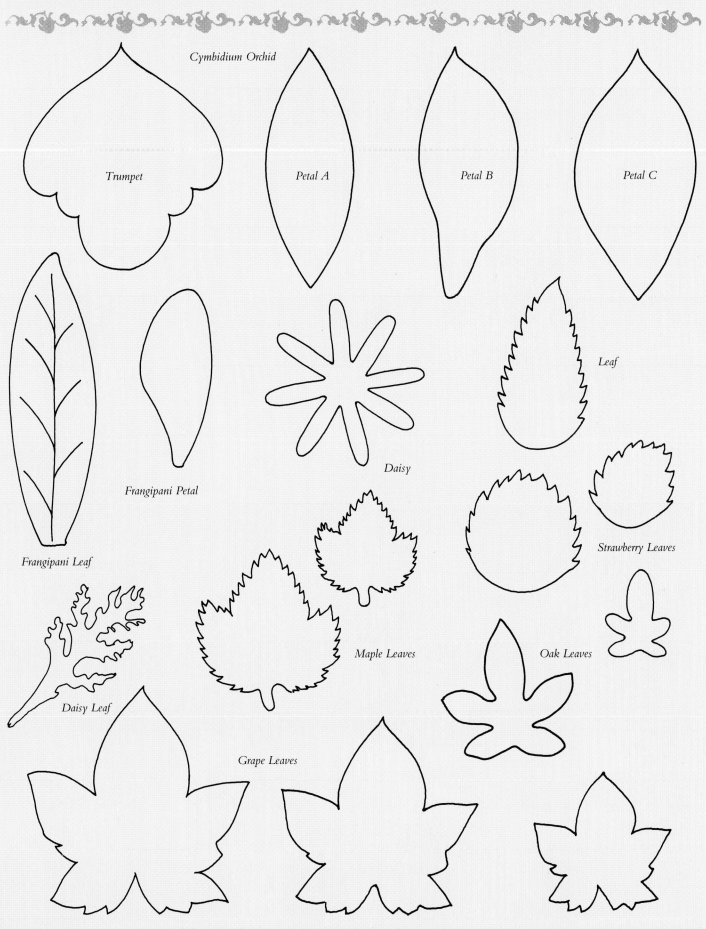

Cymbidium Orchid

Trumpet

Petal A

Petal B

Petal C

Leaf

Frangipani Petal

Daisy

Frangipani Leaf

Strawberry Leaves

Daisy Leaf

Maple Leaves

Oak Leaves

Grape Leaves

Embroidery Patterns

His and Hers

page 42

Pattern for Eyelet Embroidery

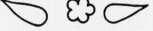

Lace Pieces

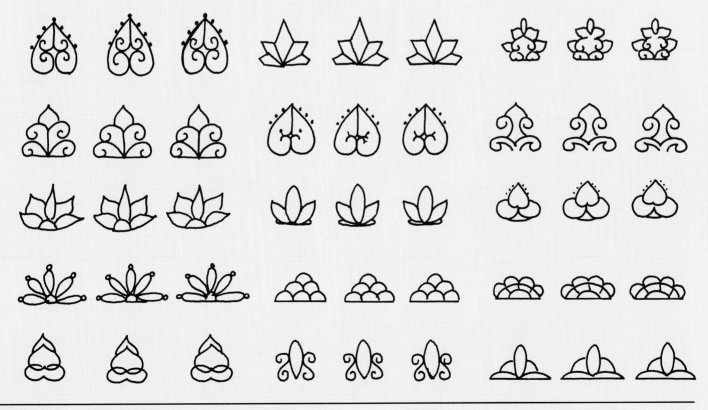

Orange Blossoms

page 48

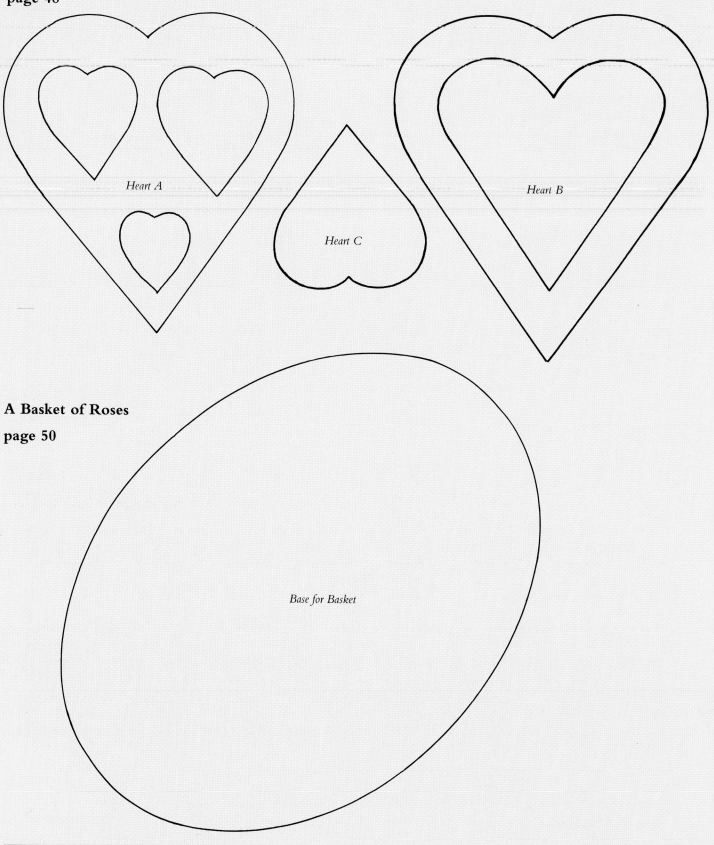

Heart A

Heart C

Heart B

A Basket of Roses

page 50

Base for Basket

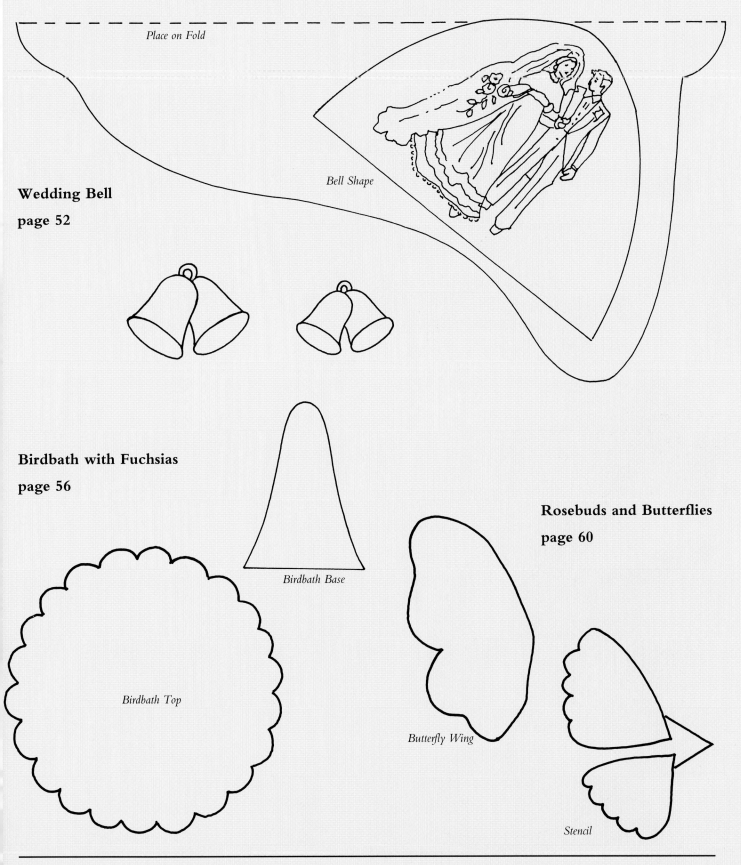

Wedding Bell

page 52

Place on Fold

Bell Shape

Birdbath with Fuchsias

page 56

Birdbath Base

Birdbath Top

Rosebuds and Butterflies

page 60

Butterfly Wing

Stencil

Horse & Carriage
page 62

Pattern for Horse

Pattern for Small Wheel

Pattern for Large Wheel

Pattern for Carriage Filigree Work

Pattern for Small Filigree Piece

Pattern for Carriage Outline

Carnation Cascade

page 54

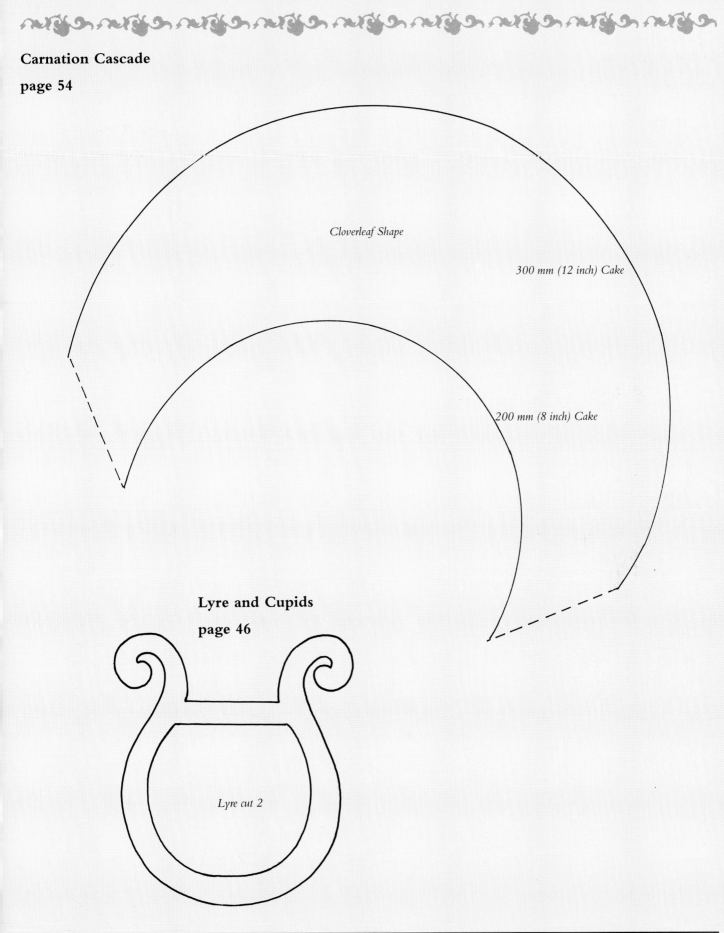

Cloverleaf Shape

300 mm (12 inch) Cake

200 mm (8 inch) Cake

Lyre and Cupids

page 46

Lyre cut 2

Make a Wish

page 64

Roof

Upright Cut 2

O

The Bride and Groom
page 40

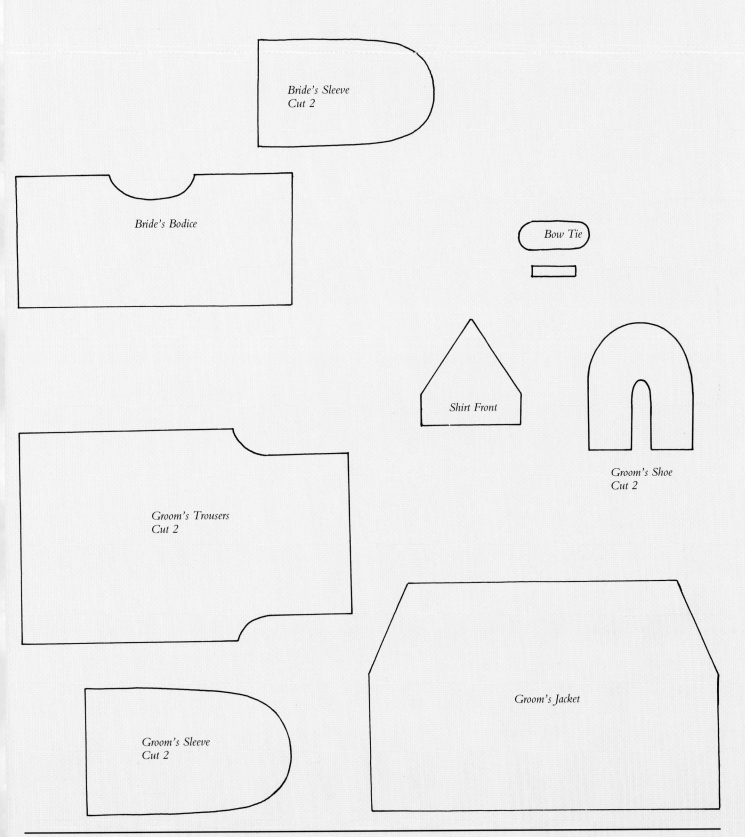

Bride's Sleeve
Cut 2

Bride's Bodice

Bow Tie

Shirt Front

Groom's Shoe
Cut 2

Groom's Trousers
Cut 2

Groom's Sleeve
Cut 2

Groom's Jacket

ABCDEFGHIJ
KLMNOPQRS
TUVWXYZ

abcdefghijklmn
opqrstuvwxyz
1234567890 &

ABCDEFGHIJKLMNOPQ
RSTUVWXYZ

Index